Handbook on Microfinance and Innovative Case Studies

Handbook on Microfinance and Innovative Case Studies

Medha Dubhashi

ALLIED PUBLISHERS PVT. LTD.

New Delhi • Mumbai • Kolkata • Chennai • Bangalore • Hyderabad

ALLIED PUBLISHERS PRIVATE LIMITED

D-5, Sector-2, **Noida**–201 301
Ph. Nos.: 0120-4320295/2542557/4352866 • E-mail: delhi.books@alliedpublishers.com

17 Chittaranjan Avenue, **Kolkata**–700072
Ph.: 033-22129618 • E-mail: cal.books@alliedpublishers.com

15 J.N. Heredia Marg, Ballard Estate, **Mumbai**–400001
Ph.: 022-42126969 • E-mail: mumbai.books@alliedpublishers.com

No. 25/10, Commander-in-Chief Road, Ethiraj Lane (Next to Post Office)
Egmore, **Chennai**–600008
Ph.: 044-28223938 • E-mail: chennai.books@alliedpublishers.com

P.B. No. 9932, No. 15, 3rd Floor (Next to Vijaya Bank), 5th Cross, Gandhinagar, Karnataka, **Bangalore**–560009, Ph.: 080-41530285 / 22386239
• E-mail: bngl.journals@alliedpublishers.com / apsabng@airtelmail.in

Sri Jayalakshmi Nilayam, No. 3-4-510, 3rd Floor (Above More Super Market)
Barkatpura, **Hyderabad**–500027
Ph.: 040-27551811, 040-27551812 • E-mail: hyd.books@alliedpublishers.com

Website: www.alliedpublishers.com

ISBN: 978-93-90951-32-1

Dedication

This book is dedicated to
my parents Padmakar and Sindhu Dubhashi
&
to Late Shivram Bhau Jadhav the "Indian Yunus"
who was the Chairman of Sindhudurg District
Central Cooperative Bank,
and under whose leadership the Bank financed
many self-help groups and helped
the people there with livelihood opportunities.

वैकुंठ मेहता राष्ट्रीय सहकारी प्रबंध संस्थान
(कृषि एवं किसान कल्याण, मंत्रालय भारत सरकार)
चतुश्रृंगी, सावित्रीबाई फुले पुणे विद्यापीठ मार्ग, पुणे – 411 007. महाराष्ट्र, भारत
VAIKUNTH MEHTA NATIONAL INSTITUTE OF CO-OPERATIVE MANAGEMENT
(Ministry of Agriculture and Farmer's Welfare, Govt. of India)
Chaturshrungi, Savitribai Phule Pune University Road, PUNE - 411 007. Maharashtra, India
कृषिगत बैंकिंग में अंतरराष्ट्रीय सहकारिता एवं प्रशिक्षण केन्द्र
चतुश्रृंगी, पुणे विद्यापीठ मार्ग, पुणे – 411 007, महाराष्ट्र, भारत
CENTRE FOR INTERNATIONAL COOPERATION & TRAINING IN AGRICULTURAL BANKING (CICTAB)
Chaturshrungi, Pune University Road, PUNE - 411 007. Maharashtra, India
(SPONSORED BY GOVT.OF INDIA AND FOOD & AGRICULTURE ORGANIZATION)

डॉ.के.के.त्रिपाठी, आई.इ.एस.
Dr.K.K.Tripathy, IES
निदेशक, वैमनीकॉम व सिक्टैब
Director, VAMNICOM & CICTAB

Foreword

It gives me immense pleasure to write foreword for the book entitled 'MICROFINANCE' by Prof. Medha Dubhashi of Vaikunth Mehta National Institute of Cooperative Management.

Planning and development in India have been concerned as much with the problems of implementation and innovative solutions that practical administrators and bankers have worked out to them as with the allocation of financial resources and equitable distribution thereof and the design of the financial programmes and schemes envisaging universal financial inclusion. The mechanisms for timely, adequate, efficient and affordable delivery of financial services are exceedingly important in ensuring that the vision of inclusive growth is made a reality.

Transformation in the banking policies and practices and the resultant improvement in the outreach and access to total bank credit during the post bank nationalization period have not satisfactorily addressed the issues of equitable and efficient delivery of agricultural and rural credit. Due to the declining public capital formation in the agricultural sector and the persistent lukewarm attitude of the rural bankers towards formal financing, the planners and policy makers are relying on microfinance to suitably supplement formal banking in rural India. This has led to witness numerous innovations being tried out by various States all across the country in the field of microfinance.

(संस्थान हिन्दी पत्राचार का स्वागत करता है।)

Ph.(O) : 020-66221400/25537974 (O)
Direct : 020-25537727/25539824
Fax : 020-25537727
E-mail : director@vamnicom.gov.in
Website : www.vamnicom.gov.in

This book, besides delineating microfinance concepts and its evolution, reviews the trend, status, issues and opportunities in micro-finance space of the economy. This book adds to the extant knowledge about microfinance sector, its potential outreach and its importance to ensure inclusive growth for all in a country like India.

I extend my sincere greetings to Prof. Dubhashi who has taken a lot of pain and brought out this book which is full of relevant case studies and apt examples on best practices in Microfinance.

I hope that this MICROFINANCE book would be a valuable input for all levels of the government administrators, research scholars, development practitioners and policy planners.

K. K. Tripathy.

Dr. K.K. Tripathy
Director (VAMNICOM)

Preface

Since the last two decades, the Self Help Groups have been recognized as important informal financial intermediaries. In India, the SHG-Bank linkage model has completed three decades and has become a successful microfinancing program. About 14 crore households have benefitted through more than 112 lakhs SHGs. The recovery of loans is remarkable at 90 per cent. Microfinancing through SHGs is providing opportunities for women, who are getting empowered socially and economically through micro economic activities. Through these businesses, they are generating incomes for their families and enabling them to come above the poverty line. They are able to send their children to school, give them nutritious food and shelter. Microfinance is helping to improve the socio economic status of the weaker sections in society.

The book itself is written in a matter of fact way. It covers the topics as per the syllabus on microfinance in most examinations. The objectives in the beginning give a guideline on what it will cover. Microfinance as a subject began to be taught only since the last 15 years or so. As such, it is difficult to find a text on the subject. While I was teaching at the post graduate level, the students were relying more on information available on the net. Except from published reports there is not much matter that is easily available. So this endeavors to write the book.

The merit of this book lies in the fact that it is perhaps the first time that the subject has been looked upon both as a text and as experiential learning through case studies of the Best Practices in Microfinance. The book has arisen out of the lectures delivered by me on the subject to the students and participants in a wide variety of courses. It is written in the conviction that it will help students and practitioners in the field of microfinance or those interested in it's study.

This book is a part of the coursework for the Diploma/Degree of various Institutes/Universities. It is divided into two parts—the basics and perspective in Microfinance and Case Studies. The first part; chapters 1 to 11, gives an overview of microfinance—concepts, features, various delivery methodologies of microfinance, issues and challenges facing the sector in India, chapters 12 to 19 are case studies and gives examples of successful microfinance models in India and South Asia.

It is a matter of privilege that the foreword has been written by Dr. K.K. Tripathy, IES, Director, Vaikunth Mehta National Institute of Cooperative Management, Pune. There could have been no better reward for my efforts than this. I am deeply grateful to him for having found time in the midst of his responsibilities.

Last but not least I would like to thank my parents, Padmakar and Sindhu Dubhashi for their perpetual guidance and constant support. I also appreciate the support from my brother Dr. Devdatt Dubhashi, Professor, Gotheborg University, Sweden. I feel overjoyed that my daughter Archana, Senior Software Engineer at Globalstar, USA suggested me ideas in bringing out this book.

This book will be useful for academicians, students, NGO and practitioners in this field.

Professor (Dr.) Medha Dubhashi
Vaikunth Mehta National Institute of
Cooperative Management, Pune

About the Author

Prof. (Dr.) Medha Dubhashi is an outstanding academician; having vast experience in training, research and teaching in India and Philippines. She was Professor and Founder-Head of Centre for Gender Studies at Vaikunth Mehta National Institute of Cooperative Management, Pune. She obtained graduate Masters degree in Commerce from Delhi University. Her Doctoral Thesis was entitled "Women Entrepreneurs in Delhi—A Socio-economic Study for the Decade 1975–85.

Her field of expertise are Microfinance, Entrepreneurship Management, Developing Methodologies and Analysis of Gender Responsive Budgeting, Gender Issues and Capacity building in cooperatives.

She worked on a CIDA project "Women Managers in Government and Non-government organizations; which was a five country effort that aimed to promote the development of South East Asian women for managerial leadership in Indonesia, Malaysia, Philippines, Singapore and Thailand.

The United Nations Working Group on the Issue of Discrimination against Women in Law and in Practice, office of the high Commissioner for Human Rights, Geneva invited her to present a paper on "Micro-Credit and Women's Cooperative".

Her paper on "Women in Cooperatives" was well acclaimed at the IAFFE conference at Stanford University, California and Sungshin Women's University, South Korea.

She has Collaborated with international organizations such as International Cooperative Alliance (ICA), International Labour Organization (ILO-Coopnet), United Nations (UN) in conducting programs on Gender Integration of Women in Cooperatives, Women Executives at Workplaces and Self-help Groups as a subsystem of Cooperatives.

Pioneered Gender Budgeting workshops in Maharashtra for government officials in various ministries. Developing methodologies for analysis of schemes of Department of Cooperation, Maharashtra.

Authored several books, articles, case studies, published in journals of repute. Papers were written on topics such as self-help groups, micro-finance, financial management, entrepreneurship, co-operation and gender issues.

Conducted national and international training programs for co-operative executives, office bearers, and senior executives including CEO, MD/GM on Microfinance in SAARC countries in collaboration with Grameen Bank, Bangladesh, Nepal Cooperative Development Corporation, Nepal and Bhutan Financial Development Corporation, Bhutan.

About 200 program have been conducted and trained more than 10000 senior cooperative personnel in State Departments and Co-operative Institutions such as banks, sugar, dairy, in number of Cooperative Management Development Programs.

Invited as expert faculty in training programs/workshops conducted by Cooperatives Pan India.

Awarded FIRST prize in all India case writing competition conducted by Indian Institute of Public Administration New Delhi on "Gender Sensitizing in Cooperatives a Case of Dairy Cooperatives."

She can be contacted on medha_dubhashi@rediffmail.com

Contents

SECTION-I

Microfinance

CHAPTER 1

Microfinance—Concept and Evolution

Learning Objectives

1. Concept and definition of microfinance
2. Evolution, credit needs of poor
3. Microfinance innovations
4. Microfinance in India
5. Learning lessons in MF lending

Microfinance

Microfinance is a term of recent origin. It coins two elements which were not included in earlier debates and concerns in rural credit. These are: i) an emphasis on savings and other financial services and ii) group dynamics in saving and lending.

Microfinance is the provision of financial services to low income people. Microfinance has it's roots in micro credit; and has evolved in recent decades. In the 1970s, social innovators from the Global South introduced the concept that small amounts of short term capita (micro credit) can help poor people in the informal economy engage in productive activities and grow their way out of poverty. The early success of micro credit demonstrated that poor families in the informal economy are valuable customers and that it is possible to serve them in large numbers in a sustainable way.

Over the last decade, the lesson learnt was that poor households need access to full range of financial services to generate income, build assets, smooth consumption and manage risks—financial services that a more limited micro credit model cannot provide. Hence the term "microfinance" generally refers to a broad set of financial services tailored to fit the needs of the poor individuals.

Micro credit is small loans given to the poorest of the poor. But microfinance includes savings, insurance and remittances. Thus it covers a range of financial services that the poor would need. It highlights the importance of savings and other financial services for poor people. According to Task Force constituted by NABARD a working definition of microfinance is "provision of thrift, credit and other financial services to the un-served poor, enabling them to raise their income levels and improve their standard of living." The proposed Microfinance Services Regulation Bill defines microfinance services as providing financial assistance to an individual or an eligible client, either directly or through a group mechanism for an amount, not exceeding Rs. 50,000 in aggregate (Rs. 1,50,000 for housing purposes).

The global financial inclusion agenda recognizes these broader needs. It also recognizes the importance of financial literacy, building consumer financial capabilities, and for consumer protection policies that take the conditions and constraints of poor families in the informal economy into account.

Micro Credit Summit 1997

On February 2–4, 1997, more than 2,900 people from 137 countries gathered at the Microcredit Summit to launch a campaign to reach 100 million of the world's poorest families, especially the women of those families, with credit for self-employment and other financial and business services by the year 2005. In a historic speech it was declared that "the time has come that micro credit is a powerful tool to end poverty and economic dependence" at the Micro Credit Summit, Ela Bhat, General Secretary Self Employed Women's Association famously said that "without the active participation of the poor, and especially poor women, poverty will not be reduced" Nancy Berry, President Women's World Banking stated that "we are in the business of social change".

Five objectives were associated with the International Year of Micro Credit:

1. Assess and promote the contribution of and microcredit to the MDGs.
2. Increase public awareness and understanding of microfinance and microcredit as vital parts of the development equation.

3. Promote inclusive financial sectors.
4. Encourage innovation and new partnerships by promoting and supporting strategic partnership to build and expand the outreach and success of microcredit and microfinance.
5. Encourage innovation and new partnerships by promoting and supporting strategic partnership to build and expand the outreach and success of microcredit and microfinance.

Sustainable Development Goals

At the Sustainable Development Summit on 25 September 2015, UN Member States adopted the 2030 Agenda for Sustainable Development, which includes a set of 17 Sustainable Development Goals (SDGs) to end poverty, fight inequality and injustice, and tackle climate change by 2030. The SDGs build on the Millennium Development Goals (MDGs), eight anti-poverty targets that the world committed to achieving by 2015. The MDGs, adopted in 2000, aimed at an array of issues that included slashing poverty, hunger, disease, gender inequality, and access to water and sanitation. Enormous progress has been made on the MDGs, showing the value of a unifying agenda. Despite this success, poverty has not ended for all.

India is a signatory to the United Nation's Sustainable Development Goals (SDGs). India needs to achieve the 17 targets and 28 indicators by 2030.

Box 1.1: SDG Goals

Consumption and Investment Needs of Poor

Poor people have consumption needs such as food, housing. Unless these primary needs are satisfied, poor will not invest in business. This is the reason that often credit given for investment purposes is misutilized. The needs of the poor can be classified as:

Life cycle needs: education, house construction, festivals, marriage, etc Emergency needs: medical emergencies, accidents, natural calamities Investment needs: Income generating assets, small business.

Credit Requirements

For the needs mentioned above, poor require access to funds. What is the source of funds?

- They could use their savings
- They could borrow
- They could resort to sale/mortgage of assets like land, valuables and livestock.

Why Don't Poor People Use Traditional Banks?

Poor people in developing countries do not qualify for services from the formal banking sector as they have no credit history, are not employed in the formal sector so there is no record of employment. Most importantly, they are unable to provide collateral. In many parts of the world opening a saving account at a traditional bank requires certain amount of money to be deposited which is not available with the poor. Yet, people living in poverty need access to a diverse range of financial services to help run a small business, manage risk and plan for a stable future. There is a dire need for financial saving products to meet the diverse needs of the poor. Formal institutions like the banks do not provide credit to the poor as they have no collateral to offer. Banks are not very enthusiastic to lend to the poor as they doubt their ability to absorb credit without first building their capacity to save. This makes the poor vulnerable to natural and manmade disasters. This gap was addressed by Professor Muhammad Yunus.

Exhibit 1.1: Nobel Laureate Professor Muhammad Yunus (right) with Dr. P.R. Dubhashi, founder Director of Vaikunth Mehta National Institute of Cooperative Management and the Author.

An innovative approach emerged during 1990s both theory in practice and backed by an emerging international consensus. The main theory was that access to money is essential to move out of poverty. People can control their own destiny if capital is linked to work. This gives poor control over their lives and eliminates poverty faster.

In 1974, Bangladesh was hit by a powerful feminine. Professor Muhammad Yunus was teaching economics at the University of Chittagong. Against the backdrop of the famine Prof. Yunus wanted to help the poor. He saw in the village of Jobra, there was a poor women making a stool made of bamboo. She had borrowed money from the money lender to whom she had to sell back the stool and get 97 cents in return. There were such 42 poor people who had borrowed a total amount of US$ 27. There was no bank that was ready to give credit to the poor because they were considered as unworthy for credit as they did not have any collateral. Unless the poor were liberated from the money lender no economic programme could stop them from alienating the poor. Credit could bring the money and allow the poor to sell their products in a free market to fetch a better spread between the cost of materials and sale price. But no formal financial institution was available to cater to the needs of the poor. The poor were unable to save and were therefore caught in a vicious circle. The poor had no financial structure which could help them widen their economic base. This led Prof Yunus to set up a Bank for the poor called "Grameen Bank".

Grameen Bank is a special bank that is owned by the borrowers themselves to facilitate social and economic development of the poor by tapping the resources which people already possess viz., their enterprise, their productive skills, and willingness to work hard to secure their survival and development. An influx of credit helped to break the vicious cycle of poverty by creating new opportunities to save and invest in income generating activities.

Exhibit 1.2: Grameen Bank, Mirpur, Dhaka, Bangladesh

What are the some ways that people use their microfinance loans?

The ways in which people use their loans varies as the way people earn a living. Some by life stock, suing machine and fabric to make clothes and accessories, stock for a local store, a tractor or seed and other farming equipment and supplies. The possibilities are endless as to what micro entrepreneur can do with his or her loan. Microfinance clients have excellent track records for repayment. Repayment rates for microfinance loans on a global level average about 97%.

Does Microfinance Help Solve Poverty?

Poverty is a complicated issue and many different approaches and tools are required to address it. Microfinance is one tool that is appropriate for millions of the poor to lift themselves out of poverty. However, microfinance is not a panacea for elimination of poverty. Despite the problems microfinance remains a popular and widely used form of development assistance.

So what are the important ethical questions round microfinance?

There are three that are central to the debate:

1. Is it ethical to do business with the poor or earn profit from poor people?
2. Is it ethical to maximize profit when doing business with the poor?
3. Do we have an ethical responsibility to avoid harming poor people in the process?

The answer to the above questions is that while you can do business with a poor maximizing profit should not be the primary focus. There should be an obligation to the poor.

Evolution of MF in India

In India a NGO called Myrada was pioneering group lending and credit. Seeing this NABARD propagated an alternative model of reaching the rural poor through informal Self help groups. The Self Help Group programme has come a long way since 1992 passing through stages of pilot (1992–1995) mainstream in (1995 to 1998) and expansion (1998 onwards) and emerged as the worlds biggest microfinance programme in terms of outreach covering 1.6 million groups and 80% of market share in India.

Box 1.2: SHG Bank Linkage Program
The Self Help Group—Bank Linkage Programme, which is the largest microfinance programme in the world, today touches: • 13.8 crores households • Through more than 112 lakhs SHGs • With deposits of about Rs. 37,477 crores • Annual Loan of Rs. 58,000 crore and • Loan outstanding of nearly Rs. 1,03,289 crores

Source: Status of Microfinance in India 2020–21, NABARD.

The task Force on Supportive Policy and Regulatory Framework for Microfinance has defined mF as the "provision of thrift, credit and other financial services and products of very small amounts to the poor in rural, semi-urban or urban areas for enabling them to raise their income levels and improve living standards". While exclusively covering the poor, it lays emphasis on helping borrowers to move from the pre-mE (micro enterprise) stage to the post-mE stage. This up scaling is done through the support of financial and non-financial services.

Lessons for MF Lending

1. The poor are bankable Lessons learnt from Grameen Bank suggested that the poor were capable of using credit profitably and repaying loans from their sales proceeds. The belief held by bankers that poor were not bankable was incorrect. Lending to the poor did not necessarily have a high risk. When the poor were involved as a group and the realization that their repayment enhanced their long term borrowing capacity, reduced the chances of default on repayment.
2 Micro credit benefitted the poor. Evidence from India and other countries showed that microfinance benefitted the poor by providing them savings opportunities and credit. Micro credit helped the poor borrowers to increase their incomes and enhanced their livelihood opportunities. Women groups had a greater sense of participation and enhanced their empowerment.
3. *Savings Mobilization Strengthened MFIs:* MFIs which mobilized saving enhanced their sustainability. Microfinance should be viewed as having two complementary components, Micro Credit and Savings.

There was a close co-relation between the success in savings mobilization and the overall success of MFIs. Apart from improving the fund base the members had a stake in the MFI and were more accountable. Savings also formed an important foundation for participatory involvement. Savings mobilization strengthened the asset base of the MFI, reduced risk, and enhanced financial viability and provided opportunities for supplementary income.

4. *Need for Strong Governance:* Good governance led to greater transparency in the activities and finances of micro insurance. Good accounting practices were essential to ensure accountability and evaluation of performance.
5. Strong regulatory framework with an expansion in the number of MFIs, there should be a strong regulatory framework in the interest of both the poor and the MFI.
6. No single model of MFI. There is no single model of successful MFI. Each MFI would have to be oriented to the needs of the particular community and increase participatory involvement, develop group action, find innovative means of reducing administration and transaction cost and increase outreach.
7. Credit alone cannot achieve objectives. Micro credit attempts to address a genuine need of credit for the poor for consumption needs, working capital and sometimes fix capital of small enterprises.

CHAPTER 2

Microfinance in India: An Overview

Learning Objectives

1. Indian rural economy
2. Poverty alleviation schemes in India
3. Transforming India—new schemes in agricultural sector
4. Agricultural credit needs
5. Credit supply alternative to money lender

Eliminating rural poverty has been a major developmental objective in third world countries. This aim figures prominently in National Plans; but few can claim to have found the right approach to the problem.

Indian Rural Economy

India is an agricultural country with 60% of the population living in rural areas. Though agriculture is the primary occupation of rural people, the income from agriculture is unstable. Hence, the trend is to move to various non-agricultural occupations. The main source of credit for farmers and people in rural areas is the money lender who charged usurious rates of interest. Banks did not give credit because the small and marginal farmers had no collateral. Rural indebtedness is a stumbling block in the way of rural prosperity. It is one of the biggest and most serious problem of India's rural economy. Indebtedness means an obligation to return the money from whom it was borrowed. Rural indebtedness is an indicator of the weak infrastructure in our country; which reflects the inability of our economic system to reach the needy farmers. The causes of rural indebtedness may be due to anyone or several of the following reasons.

1. Low income
2. Illiteracy and poverty
3. Unproductive expenditure on marriage, litigation etc.
4. Inherited debt
5. Unpredictable monsoon
6. Exploitation by money lenders.

Consequences of Rural Indebtedness

Rural indebtedness is a major reason for the farmers suicide across a number of states. In most cases the economic status of the farmer; being a small and marginal farmer was very poor. Secondly, after the green revolution agricultural activities have become cash based and required high investment in inputs like seeds and fertilizers and wage labor. This is the reason for progressive states having a high incidence of farmers' suicides. Thirdly, liberalization and globalization led to a shift in cropping patterns from staple crops to cash crops like oilseeds and cotton requiring high investment and increased credit needs. In such a scenario when the prices decline farmers have no means to supplement the income.

Poverty Alleviation Programmes in India

In the 1970s as a welfare state the government introduced many schemes to uplift the poor. To help them subsidized targeted credit was provided. Directed Agricultural Credit was synonymous with rural development finance. In 1969, 14 commercial banks were nationalized. This was an attempt to make banking for masses than banking for classes. As a result, there was massive expansion of branch network in rural areas, mandatory directed credit to priority sector areas, subsidized rates of interest and the set up of regional rural banks and NABARD. These measures resulted in increased rural outreach and volume of credit. But these attempts of directed credit failed to deliver the expected results in terms of poverty alleviation. In the sixth five year plan the government launched several poverty alleviation programs like Integrated Rural Development Programs (IRDP), Training of Rural Youth for Self-Employment (TRYSEM), Development of Women and Children in Rural Areas (DWCRA), National Rural Employment Program (NREP) and Rural Landless Employment Guarantee Program (RLEGP). The government interventions like IRDP failed to deliver to the poor. As a result the institutional structure was neither optimum in rural lending nor serving the needs of the poor people. The success achieved in implementation of government supported self employment schemes was a mixed one. In spite of RBIs regulations mandating bank lending for these schemes, the targeted poor were not able to avail credit for the sustainability of their micro enterprises.

Box 2.1: Golden Moments		
1969	–	Nationalization of banks
1982–84	–	Launching of Farmers Club (Vikas Volunteer Vahini) program Propagation of Principles of Development through Credit
1986–90	–	Introduction of Potential Linked Credit Plans(PLPs)
1992–93	–	Pilot project on SHG-Bank Linkage
1993–96	–	Launching of District Rural Industries Project (DRIP)
1998–2000	–	Launching of Cluster Development Program Setting up of Microfinance Development Fund
2004–05	–	Pilot project on joint Liability Groups (JLGs)
2006–07	–	Launching of Micro Enterprise Development program
2008–09	–	Setting up of Financial Inclusion Fund(FIF) and Finncial Inclusion technology Fund (FITF)
2010–12	–	Program to engage 150 lakh poor households in 150 backward districts

Transforming India

The last two years have seen remarkable changes in India's development paradigm. India is changing from an agrarian rural society into a society with an economy dominated by the industry and services sector. More than 50% of population was in agriculture in 2004, and contributed 20% of the GDP. However by 2020 it is estimated that the population dependent on agriculture would drop to less than 30%; although the absolute population is expected to increase from 110 crores in 2004 to 120 crores in 2020.

The transformation process is as a result of increased urbanization. More people are migrating to cities and towns from rural areas. There is an increasing trend of more people being classified as urbanites. This will have its own problems such as massive growth of slums, unemployment, unsafe sanitation and hygiene, diseases and declining public health.

Further agriculture is becoming increasingly mechanized. Agriculture in India, has silently gone through a far reaching change in the past few decades. The share of human power available for carrying out a myriad operations in farming has shrunk to a mere 5%. The share of draught animals, the iconic oxen pulling the plough, has fallen to 5%. More than 90% of the power is drawn from mechanical solutions; like tractors and power tillers provide the bulk accounting to 47%, Electric motors 27%, and diesel engines 16%.

In 1971–72, 60% of the power was provided by humans and animals, 15% by farm laborers, and 45% by animals. In about two decades, in 91–92, the collective share fell to 26%, in which labor accounted for 9%, Tractors made the biggest stride from a mere 7% to 47%.

New Schemes in agricultural sector:

1. ***Pradhan Mantri Jan Dhan Yojana (PMJDY):*** Pradhan Mantri Jan-Dhan Yojana (PMJDY) is National Mission for Financial Inclusion to ensure access to financial services, namely, Banking/Savings & Deposit Accounts, Remittance, Credit, Insurance, Pension in an affordable manner. Account can be opened in any bank branch or Business Correspondent (Bank Mitr) outlet. Accounts opened under PMJDY are being opened with Zero balance. Its slogan is "Mera Khata Bhagya Vidhata".
2. ***Pradhan Mantri Fasal Bima Yojana (PMFBY):*** It is a crop insurance scheme for assisting farmers in receiving monetary assistance in the event of crop damage due to natural calamities. The farmers have to pay low premium for getting the insurance.

   There is a uniform premium of only 2% to be paid by the farmers for all kharif crops and 1.5% for all Rabi crops. The balance premium will be paid by Government to provide full insured amount to the farmers against crop loss on account of natural calamities.
3. ***Pradhan Mantri Suraksha Bima Yojana (PMSBY):*** Rs. 2.00 lakh of accident insurance for a premium of Rs. 12/- per year between the age 18 to 70 year. The accident insurance scheme will have one year cover from June 1 to May 31 and would be offered through banks and administered through public sector general insurance companies. This scheme will be linked to the bank accounts opened under the Pradhan

Mantri Jan Dhan Yojana scheme. Most of these account had zero balance initially. The government aims to reduce the number of such zero balance accounts by using this and related schemes. Now all Bank account holders can avail this facility through their net-banking service facility at any time of the year.

4. ***Pradhan Mantri Jivan Jyoti Bima Yojana (PMJJBY):*** Rs. 2.00 lakh life insurance at Rs. 330/- premium per year between the age group 18 to 50 years. The scheme will be a one year cover, renewable from year to year, Insurance Scheme offering life insurance cover for death due to any reason.
5. ***Atal Pension Yojana (APY):*** The Government of India has announced a new scheme called Atal Pension Yojana (APY). APY is a guaranteed pension scheme and is administered by the Pension Fund Regulatory and Development Authority (PFRDA). Rs. 1000/- deposit between age group 18 to 60 years.
6. ***Paramparagat Krishi Vikas Yojana:*** This scheme was launched with a view to address the critical importance of soil and water for improving agricultural production.
7. ***Krishi Amdani Beema Yojana:*** This scheme was introduced with a view of the following points:
   (a) To give an impetus to the dying agricultural practice.
   (b) There is 14 crore hectares of agri land in India, of which only 44% is under irrigation.
   (c) This yojana was taken considering the plight of small and marginal farmers who were leaving the agricultural practice because of the uncertainty over the produce and returns.
   (d) It was introduced so that the farmers do not bear any financial burden if their produce gets destroyed due to unexpected weather of for any other reason.
8. ***Pradhan Mantri Gram Sinchai Yojana:*** Ensure water supply to farmers round the year. Irrigation project would be selected for releasing funds by the state government after seeking nod of the concerned Zilla Parishad.
9. ***Pradhan Mantri Sansad Adarsh Gram Yojana:*** It was developed for the development of Model village. Under this Yojana, members of parliament will be responsible for developing the socio-economic and physical infrastructure of 3 villages each by 2019 and a total of 8

villages each by 2024. This implies that a total of 6433 Adarsh gram of the 265000 gram panchyats will be created by 2024.

Key Objectives of the Yojana: The selection of villages by the MPs must be any village other than their own village. The village must be of a population of 3000–5000 people if it is located in the plans or 1000:3000 people is located in hilly areas.

The funds for this scheme must be raised from Indira Awas Yojana, Pradhan Mantri Gram Sadak Yojana, Mahatma Gandhi National rural employment guarantee scheme, and backward regions Grand fund etc. The members of parliaments local area development scheme etc.

10. ***PM-KISAN Scheme:*** The PM-Kisan scheme is a flagship scheme of the Central government, launched in February 2019. Under the scheme, an income support of Rs. 6000 per year is provided to small and marginal farmers, having land holdings upto 2 hectares (nearly 5 acres). Its ambit was slowly extended to all farmers with certain exclusions under Modi 2.0 Accordingly over 14 crore landholder farmers in the country are eligible to receive Rs. 6000 each per annum in three equal installments of Rs. 2000 directly into their bank accounts. On the national level, Rs. 1.15 lakh crore have been directly sent to the bank accounts of more than 10.75 crore farmers.

    Government data on the flagship scheme, shows that almost one fourth beneficiaries among landholder farmers in the country are women. Further northeastern states and Kerala are taking the lead in bridging the gap of gender disparities. Smallest number of women beneficiaries at 52 (11.35% of the total 458).

Table 2.1: Top Five States with Maximum Beneficiaries

State	*Men in Crores*	*Women in Crores*
Uttar Pradesh	1.89	42.72
Maharashtra	82.83	19.87
Madhya Pradesh	61.13	15.83
Bihar	50.73	21.52
Rajasthan	41.72	22.70

Source: Government data upto September 7th as per RTI reply.

Uttar Pradesh is the topper for both genders. Maharashtra, Madhya Pradesh, Bihar, and Rajasthan top the list of states with largest number of male beneficiaries. After Uttar Pradesh, Rajasthan, Bihar, Maharashtra account for the largest number of women beneficiaries.

If we look at nationwide figures, 2.46 crores (24.25%) are women beneficiaries; while 7.70 crores (75.75%) are men.

Table 2.2: Region-wise Total Beneficiaries

Region	*North*	*South*	*Central*	*East*	*West*	*Northeast*
In %	28.57	21.72	10.21	12.47	22.03	3.91
In crores	2.90	2.20	1.03	1.26	2.24	39.73

Source: Government data upto September 7th as per RTI reply.

As per RTI data till September 7th, total 10.05 crores beneficiaries in 27 states and 11.14 lakhs in 9 UTIs received money into their bank accounts. After election West Bengal has recently been included in the Scheme.

The North eastern states showed gender parity; while big states like Uttar Pradesh, Maharashatra, and Bihar lagged behind. Out of the 1.64 beneficiaries in Meghalay, 63.51% are women. Meghalaya has the highest percentage of women beneficiaries among all states and Union Terrioteries. In Nagaland 52.61%, Manipur 54.35%, and Arunachal Pradesh 51.98% women accounted for more than 50% of the beneficiaries.

Far away, Lakshwadeep sends a strong message as women make up a significant 49.41% of the total 1789 beneficiaries. Among other states, Kerala accounts for 40% women beneficiaries. The state accounts for 44.20% of the over 33.46 lakh beneficiaries.

Uttar Pradesh has the maximum number of beneficiaries (1,89 crores men and 42.72 women), followed by Maharashtra (82.83 lakh men and 19.87 lakh women).

In nine states and Union Terrioteries including Bihar, Telangana, Gujrat, Karnataka, Odisha, Chattisgarh, Jharkhand,, Madhya Pradesh, Dadar and Nager Haveli, Daman and Dui women accounted for 20–30% of total beneficiaries.

In seven states and UTs including Mizoram, Puducherry, Anadaman and Nicobar islands, Rajasthan, Andhra Pradesh, Assam and Tamil Nadu women accounted for 30–40% of beneficiaries; making it more than the national average.

11. ***Pradhan Mantri Mudra Yojana:*** Micro Units Development and Refinance Agency (MUDRA) is an NBFC supporting development of micro enterprise sector in the country. MUDRA provides refinance support to banks/MFIs for lending to micro units having loan requirement upto 10 lakhs. MUDRA provides refinance to micro business under the scheme of Pradhan Mantri MUDRA Yojana. To signify the stage of growth/development and funding needs of the beneficiary micro units/entrepreneur, MUDRA offers incentives through the following interventions:
    (a) *Shishu:* Covering loans upto 50,000
    (b) *Kishor:* Covering loans above 50,000 and upto 5 lakhs
    (c) *Tarun:* Covering loans above 5 lakhs and upto 10 lakhs.

    Generally, loans upto 10 lakhs issued by banks under Micro Small Enterprises is given without collaterals.

    Objective of the Scheme: Mudra loan is extended for a variety of purposes which provide income generation and employment creation. The loans are extended mainly for:
    - Business loans for Vendors, traders, shopkeepers and other service sector activities.
    - Working capital loan through Mudra cards.
    - Equipment Finance for Micro units.

12. ***PM Street Vendor's Atma Nirbhar Nidhi (PM SVANidhi) programme:*** Launched in June 2020, to help vendors amid the pandemic, the PM SVANidhi scheme is a micro credit facility that provides street vendors a collateral-free loan of Rs. 10,000 for a year at concessional rates of 7,25%. It was envisioned to help daily wage workers, many of them migrant laborers, who suffered during the lockdown. All vendors who were vending since March 24, 2020, and had a certificate of vending, could avail of the loan. On timely repayment of the loan, an interest subsidy at 7% per annum is credited to the bank accounts of beneficiaries through Direct Benefit Transfer on a six monthly basis.

    According to the data available with the Ministry of Housing and Urban Affairs, there are 42.7 lakhs street vendors in the country; excluding West Bengal. Uttar Pradesh (7.5 lakh), followed by

Maharashtra (5.7 lakh), Telangana (5.7 lakh), Madhya Pradesh (5 lakh), Gujarat (3.6 lakh), and Andhra Pradesh (2.7 lakh) has the highest number of street vendors (till date 24.2.2021).

Ever since the scheme was launched, a total of 37 lakh loan applications were received; and 20 lakh have been sanctioned. Uttar Pradesh tops in disbursing vendor loans, in disbursing of 3.5 lakh loans. Madhya Pradesh and Telangana have given out over 2 lakh loans; West Bengal, Assam and Kerala have disbursed only a small fraction of those numbers PSU banks account for 95 per cent of the loans sanctioned. However, despite this interest subvention—making this an effectively interest-free loan-many accounts have turned NPAs. The total non-performing asset (NPA) rate under the scheme was 7 per cent.

As per the guidelines, Urban Local Bodies (ULBs) and Town Vending Committees (TVCs) are responsible for identifying eligible borrowers and issue Certificate of Vending, Identity card and Letter of Recommendation to them. As of January 2021, bank disbursements were made to 13.27 lakh beneficiaries, with Rs. 1306.76 crore worth of loans disbursed.

13. ***Soil Health Card Scheme:*** For every farmer deterioration of soil health, sub optional u incentivestilization of farming resources, Imbalanced use of fertilizers, low addition of organic matter and non-replacement of depleted micro and secondary nutrients is a cause of concern. Soil health need to be assessed from time to time; so that the farmers can apply for the required nutrients already present in the soil. Government has launched the scheme to provide every farmer a soil health card. This card will carry crop wise recommendation of nutrient fertilizers required for farms making it possible for farmers to improve soil productivity. This scheme will provide all 145 million farm owners in the country with a soil health card for the next 3 years.

    Applying fertilizers, best quality seed and ample water is not enough. Farmers should nurture their soil and know what inputs to use and in what quantities. The agriculture ministry released Rs. 86 crore for the soil health card scheme.

Agricultural Credit

- "The Indian peasant is born in debt, lives in debt and bequeaths the indebtedness to his successor"—The Royal Commission on Agriculture (1928).
- Agricultural Credit need arises because the personal resources of the farmers are inadequate to meet the costly farm technology. Credit requirements of the farmers may be classified as a) credit for Productive and unproductive purpose and b) on Time period Basis. Productive Purpose include activities which help in the improvement of agricultural productivity such as purchase of inputs like seeds and raw material and permanent improvements in land. Unproductive credit needs may include social and religious functions, celebration of marriages, litigation.
- Credit required for productive purpose can be divided broadly into following categories:
  (a) *Short Term (for periods upto 15 months):* Short term loans are required for purchasing seeds and fertilizers, labour charges etc. Mostly, they are repaid after the harvest.
  (b) *Medium Term (from 15 months to 5 years):* Medium term loans are granted for purposes such as sinking of well, purchase of bullocks and implements).
  (c) *Long Term (above 5 years):* Loans repayable over longer periods are utilized for payment of old debts, making permanent improvements in the farm or increasing the size of holding, purchase of heavy machinery such as tractors.

Sources of Credit

Sources of Agricultural Credit are grouped as:

(a) ***Institutional Sources:*** Include cooperative societies, commercial banks and other government agencies.
(b) ***Non-Institutional Sources:*** Include moneylenders, landlords, relatives etc.

Institutional Arrangements

Agriculture credit is disbursed through a multi agency network which includes commercial banks, regional rural banks and cooperatives. With their vast network and wide coverage and outreach, the cooperative credit institutions are the main institutional mechanism for agricultural credit.

A major issue relating to agricultural credit is difficulty to access institutional credit. The poor do not want subsidies, but access to credit. They want reliable and continuous access to financial services. Though they borrow small amounts, but these tiny loans have a huge impact. A small loan can make a big difference in their lives and their work. The poor use their loans for a mix of family needs and enterprise. Wherever quality SHGs are promoted, loan recovery climate has perceptibly improved. Therefore, there is an urgent need to sensitize all the key officials of cooperative banks as also the senior officials of Cooperation Department of the state governments to the SHG bank linkage program.

Problems of Rural Finance

Bankers hesitate to lend to rural population due to several reason.

1. ***Uncertainty and Risk of Default:*** Bank lending to farmers is surrounded by uncertainty about repayment. The agricultural income is irregular with volatile income streams and expenditure patterns. They also tend to be highly exposed to systemic risk such as crop failures, fall in commodity price. So banks tend to perceive such loans as risky.
2. ***High Transaction Cost:*** The transaction cost is high due to small loan sizes, high frequency of transactions, large geographical spread, heterogeneity of borrowers and wide spread illiteracy. Moreover, private sector banks lack rural branch network.
3. ***Lack of Credit Information:*** Problem caused by uncertainty are exacerbated by the lack of reliable information on the past credit history of borrowers. The credit information bureaus do not focus on small rural borrowers. Credit information on such borrowers is difficult to obtain because the majority of the rural poor rely on money lender and informal lender.
4. ***Difficulties of Collateral:*** The rural poor have no fixed collateral. The small plots of land often cannot be mortgaged. Identification of alternative collateral is costly and cumbersome. Most banks extend loan only if they have collateral. Hence, it is called "Banking with Collateral"; is a serious constrain to lending to farmers.

5. ***Week Legal Framework and Enforcement:*** Government has not been able to develop and enforce a legal and regulatory framework conducive to rural finance. Land titling and registration systems are weak and the use and transfer of land is difficult. Many states do not permit leasing of land, while in some states the lesse creates long term irrevocable rights to the disadvantages of the lessor.
6. ***Lack of Proper Government Policies:*** The government's policy have made things worse from the bank's perspective creating a "financial climate" not conducive to lending in general and rural banking in particular.

Microfinance Program in India

The biggest microfinance program in the world is run in India. About 4 crore people are accessing micro credit and micro financial services.

Table 2.3: Data on SHG Bank Linkage

S. No.		*Physical No in Lakhs*	*Financial R in Crores*
1.	Total number of SHGs saving linked with banks	112.23	37,477.61
	(a) Out of total SHGs—exclusive Women SHGs	97.25	32,686.08
	(b) Out of total SHGs—under NRLM/SGSY	64.78	19,353.70
	(c) Out of total SHGs—under NULM/SJSRY	5.29	1,954.09
2.	Total number of SHGs credit linked during the year 2020–21	28.87	58,070.68
	(a) Out of total SHGs—exclusive Women SHGs	25.90	54,423.13
	(b) Out of total SHGs—under NRLM/SGSY	15.84	29,643.04
	(c) Out of total SHGs—under NULM/SJSRY	1.13	2,112.04
3.	Total number of SHGs having loans outstanding as on 31 March 2021	57.80	103289.71
	(a) Out of total SHGs—exclusive Women SHGs	53.11	96,596.60
	(b) Out of total SHGs—under NRLM/SGSY	33.78	57,336.62
	(c) Out of total SHGs—under NULM/SJSRY	2.23	4,056.45
4.	Average loan amount outstanding/SHG as on 31 March, 2021 (in ₹)		178,694.37
5.	Average loan amount disbursed/SHG during 2020–21 (in ₹)		201,117.96
6.	Estimated number of families covered upto 31 March, 2021	1388	
7.	No. of Banks and Financial Institutions submitted MIS (in number)	399	

Source: Status of Micro Finance in India 2020–21, NABARD.

Inspite of the nationalization of banks, till 1990s, a large section of the rural population was unbanked. Most of the rural population took recourse to informal sources for credit. The advantage was in having flexible terms and ease in obtaining loans for consumption needs such as marriage and other purposes. With least documentation and accessibility credit was available at any time. As a result, the money lenders in the village were the last resort to many villagers whose needs were urgent and who did not hesitate to pay exorbitant interest rates without paying any heed to the disastrous consequences like coercive recovery of their productive assets; thereby pushing them into an abyss of poverty. Despite the efforts of the Government in creating and supporting an enabling environment for increasing the outreach of formal financial services to cover the marginalized population, the informal sector still played a dominant role in the village.

The spread of SHGs on an All India level is depicted in the chart below:

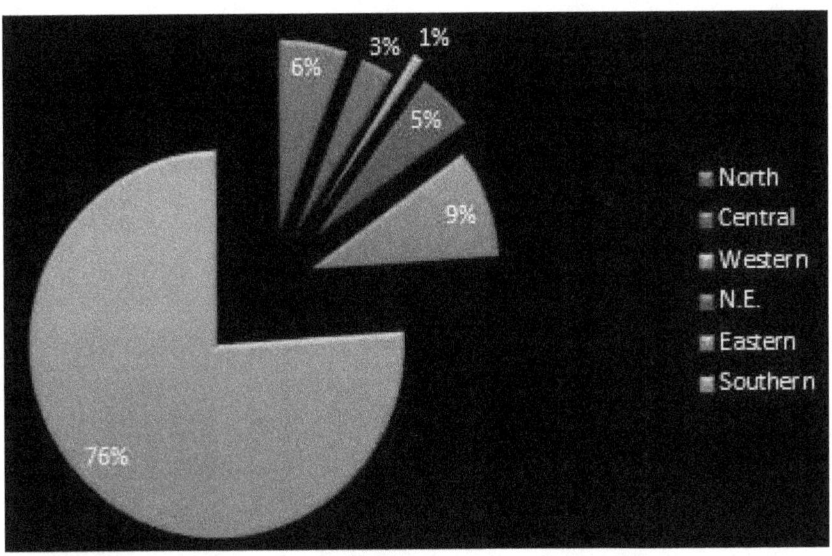

Fig. 2.1: Cumulative Bank Loans to SHGs in Regional Perspective

An important reason for the dominance of the money lender was that he had knowledge of the village and its people; whereas the commercial banks had no local knowledge. There was an information asymmetry. Further the money lender had the monopoly of door step availability of credit at the time of crisis. At this point, the Self Help Group concept emerged as a viable alternative to the money lender as it combined the flexibility and availability of informal sources with the transparency of institutional credit.

CHAPTER 3

Process of Self Help Group Formation

Learning Objectives

1. Stages in Self Help Groups formation
2. Functions of Self Help Groups
3. Features of Self Help Groups
4. SHG – Bank Linkage – Models
5. Strategy to promote SHGs
6. Self Help Group Promotion Institutions (SHPIs)

What are Self Help Groups?

Self Help Groups (SHGs) are small groups of poor people. They are informal groups of people who come together for a specific purpose. The practice of "Bhishi" in South Asia is quite common; where women come together to pool together the money collected and disburse it to one of their members. The idea behind SHG is also the same. The objective of SHG formation was to inculcate the habit of savings among the poor women mainly in rural India.

Formation of SHGs

Different methods are used in identification of the needy and the poor. Such criteria include aspects such as:

1. Women only groups.
2. Residents of same locality. The group members should preferably be from the same area, so that they can attend the meetings regularly.
3. It is advantageous if SHG members from remote villages come together.

Participatory Rural Appraisal (PRA)

- Some NGOs use "Participatory Rural Appraisal" by which the entire history of the village, the problems faced by the villagers and also the wealth ranking of villagers is ascertained. Households are asked about their family income, no. of children, education levels etc. Many groups are formed around a common cause or need which has been earlier identified. They help each other, to solve their problems.
- *Household survey: Economic variables* such as income, assets or net worth are measured.
- For example, SHARE forms groups based on per capita income or land holding. PRADHAN – uses a non-measurement approach such as peer selection.

Other Parameters Could Include

- Are the children going to school? A group can be formed on the attribute of school going children. This inadvertently encourages women wanting to join a SHG to send their children to school.
- No alcoholic husband this again encourages women SHG members whose husbands don't drink to be members of SHG.
- Low hemoglobin Very often, women from rural areas have low hemoglobin. Women are enlightened about taking a nourishing diet which includes green and leafy vegetables to increase their hemoglobin levels. Women are encouraged to grow leafy vegetables in their back garden.

Homogeneity vs. Heterogeneity

While forming groups, it must be ensured that the members have a homogeneous background. Homogeneity can be in terms of economic status, caste, gender, occupation, or commonality of interest. Members are of the same economic status. Similarly separate groups of women and men are formed to keep the homogeneity in the group. While homogeneity helps in group formation, heterogeneity enhances the functioning of the group, strong leadership, entrepreneurship and growth.

Size of the SHG

The ideal size of an SHG is 10 to 20 members; from a homogenous class who come together to address common issues. They are involved in savings and thrift activities on a regular basis and use the pooled resources in making interest bearing loans to the members of the group.

(Advantage: In a bigger group, members cannot actively participate. Also, legally it is required that an informal group should not be of more than 20 people)

Smaller the group, tighter is the inter-group linkage and more effective.

Less than 5 members, have problems in mobilizing adequate savings to meet the demands of members.

The group need not be registered.

Initial Problems

Formation of SHGs is not a smooth affair. Local coteries may hinder the formation of SHGs. Similarly tribal areas have their own customs and practices. For example in Nagaland, different tribes do not allow women to actively participate in formal bodies.

Resistance from local moneylenders. The Moneylender has a strong presence in the village, hence his resistance is the strongest. In case of women, husbands or in-laws. It is important that the women have the support of their families.

Who Helps to Form SHGS?

A reasonably educated and helpful local person has to initially help the poor people to form groups. He or she tells them about the benefits of thrift and the advantages of forming groups. The person is called an 'animator' or 'facilitator'.

Animator

Any of the following persons can be a successful animator:

- Retired school teacher or a retired government servant, who is well known locally.
- A health worker/a field officer/staff of a development agency or department of the State Government.
- The field officer or a staff member of a commercial bank/regional rural bank or a field staff from the local co-operative bank or society can also help the poor in forming groups).

- A field level functionary of an NGO.
- An unemployed educated local persons, having an inclination to help others.
- A member/participant in the Vikas Volunteer Vahini (VVV) Programme of NABARD.
- Usually, one of the following agencies help:
    1. A voluntary agency or Non Governmental Organisation (NGO)
    2. The development department of the State Government.
    3. The local branch of a bank.
- Women animators can play more effective role in organizing women SHGs. The animator cannot organize the groups all alone. He or she will need guidance, training, reading materials, etc.

Membership

From one family, only one person can become a member of an SHG. (More families can join SHGs this way.) The group normally consists of either only men or of only women. Mixed groups are generally not preferred. Women's groups are generally found to perform better. (They are better in savings and they usually ensure proper use of loans.)

- Common Living Conditions for the Group Members.
- Living in *kutcha* houses.
- Having no access to safe drinking water.
- Having no sanitary latrine.
- Those who have only one or no one employed in the family.
- Presence of illiterate adults in the family.
- Presence of an alcoholic or drug addict in the family or a member suffering permanently from prolonged illness.
- Presence of children below five years in the family.
- Family eating two meals or less a day.
- Scheduled Caste or Scheduled Tribe Families.

  (If a family has at least four of the above 9 common living conditions, it can be considered poor, and one member of that family can be encouraged to become a member of an SHGs.)

Meetings

The Group should meet regularly. Ideally, the meetings should be weekly or at least monthly.
(Advantage: They become closer, if they meet regularly. This helps them to understand each other's difficulties better.)

The Group must maintain a Weekly/Fortnightly/Monthly Register with the summary of receipts and payments. It must be updated in every meeting.

Major Functions of an SHG

Savings and Thrift

All SHG Members regularly save a small amount. The amount may be small, but savings have to be a regular and continuous habit with all the members

"Savings first – Credit later" should be the motto of every SHG member.

SHG members take a step towards self-dependence when they start small savings.

They learn financial discipline through savings and internal lending. (Advantage: This is useful when they use bank loans.) They imbibe the essentials of financial intermediation and also the basics of account keeping.

Internal Lending

Internal Lending: The SHG use the savings amount for giving loans to members. After saving for a minimum period of 2 to 3 months, the common savings fund is used by the SHG for lending to its own members. The purpose, amount, rate of interest, schedule of repayment etc., is decided by the group itself. Proper accounts has to be kept by the SHG.

Social Problems

Discussing Problems: In every meeting, the SHG members are encouraged to discuss and try to find solutions to the problems faced by them. Individually, the poor people are weak and lack resources to solve their problems. When the group tries to help its members, it becomes easier for them to face the difficulties and come up with solutions.

Loaning

Taking Bank Loan: The SHG takes loan from the bank and gives it as loan to its members.

Functions of Self Help Groups

How is an SHG Relevant?

Very poor people can save small amounts. Like the little drops of water making an ocean, their savings will slowly grow into large sums. In some branches, such savings have become lakhs of rupees.

- Maintaining large number of small savings accounts is difficult for the branch. It is also difficult to keep very small loan accounts. By opening an account for the group, the bank allows about 20 persons to save in a single account. For the Bank costs are less and time is saved. Banking with a larger number of people enables banks to gain goodwill.
- On the other hand, the Group as a whole commits repayment of the loan to the bank. Moral pressure is exerted on the borrowing members for repayment of loan. For example if a borrower defaults on payment, all the other members go to the defaulter's place and talk to her about the reasons for not repaying; and encourage her to repay the amount. Because of this, the repayment of loans by the SHGs is almost cent percent. Thus, SHGs provide good business opportunities to banks; as they provide better margins to the banks.

Repayment of Loan by the SHG

A repayment schedule is drawn up with the SHG, and the loan is to be repaid regularly. Small and frequent installments are better than large installments covering a long period.

The group members are collectively responsible for the repayment of loans to the bank. It has been the experience of bankers who lend to SHGs that the repayments from SHGs are far better when compared to individual accounts.

List of Documents for Lending to SHGs

1. Inter-se Agreement to be executed by all the members of the Self Help Group. This is an agreement by the members with the bank,

authorizing a minimum of three members to operate the group's account with the bank.

2. Application is submitted by SHG to bank branch while applying for loan assistance. This includes details of the purposes for which the SHG gives loan to its members.
3. Articles of Agreement for use by the bank while financing SHGs. This contains the duly stamped agreement between the bank and the SHG wherein both the parties agree to abide by the terms and conditions set thereon.

Linking of SHGs to Bank

Once the group is stabilized, over a period of six months, and showed mature financial behavior, it is considered for linking to banks by linking SHGs with the formal credit agencies, the poor are able to meet their credit needs. The focus under SHG-Bank Linkage Program is largely on those rural poor who have no access to the formal banking system. The target group, therefore, broadly comprise small and marginal farmers, agricultural and non agricultural labourers, artisans, craftsmen and other poor engaged in small businesses. Banks are encouraged to provide loans to SHGs in multiples of the accumulated savings of the SHGs. Loans are given without any collateral and at interest rates decided by the Bank. In turn, the groups decide the terms and conditions of loan to their members. The social dynamics and peer pressure ensures timely repayment and is social collateral for the bank loans. SB A/c in the name of SHG is opened after obtaining from the group the following documents:

Resolution from the SHG

The SHG has to pass a resolution in the group meeting, signed by all members, indicating their decision to open SB A/c with the bank. This resolution should be filed with the bank.

Authorization from the SHG

The SHG should authorize at least three members, any two of whom, to jointly operate upon their account. The resolution along with the filled in application form duly introduced by the promoter may be filed with the bank branch.

Copy of the Rules and Regulations of the SHG

This is not a must. If the group has not formulated any such rules or regulations, loans can be sanctioned without them.

After six months, if the SHG satisfies the bank as per the check list for quality; bank can give loans to the SHG. A savings bank account passbook is issued to the SHG. This is in the name of the SHG and not in the name of any individual/s.

Models of SHG Bank Linkage

Model I: *Bank – SHG – Members*

In this model the bank itself promotes and nurtures the self-help groups until they reach maturity.

Model II: *Bank – Facilitating Agency – SHG – Members*

Here groups are formed and supported by NGOs or government agencies.

Exhibit 3.1: Consumer Store Set-up by SHG Members, Sindhudurgh, Maharashtra

Model III: *Bank – NGO – mFI – SHG – Members*

In this model NGOs act as both facilitators and micro-finance intermediaries. The NGOs in turn have been found to federate SHGs into apex organizations to facilitate inter-group lending and larger access to funds.

SHG Bank Linkage Programme Present and Future

The program has been providing the rural poor access to the formal banking system and has achieved several milestones in terms of gender sensitization, empowerment and poverty alleviation. The program provides thrift linked credit support to the members of SHGs. The SHGs financing is also been included in priority sector lending. Recoveries from loans to SHGs is near 100 per cent, making them the most secure risk adjusted priority sector lending.

While the program directly benefits the members, it also helps banks in reducing their transaction costs and risk in delivering small loans. The program assumed the form of a microfinance movement and made inroads in resource poor regions.

Over the years, SHG lending by cooperative banks years has lost pace and is plateauing. This 2 decade old programme was initiated by the NABARD in 1992. Initially, it started slowly but showed a steady growth over a period. Cooperative banks were encouraged to own up SHG-Bank linkage as a business opportunity to expand their business portfolio with quality clients.

However, in the last 3 years pace of linkage has slowed down due to number of factors. It suffered due to introduction of subsidies, poor quality of groups, defaults and high dropout rates. SHG promotion did not have adequate investment. Building SHGPI capacity also did not take place. Further, there was no clear consensus between NABARD and NRLM. Government is also setting National Women Bank for SHG Financing. Reserve Bank of India issued stringent regulatory guidelines. Many controversies were raised post the Andhra Pradesh crisis. In the absence of Micro Finance Act, there was lot of uncertainty among banks whether to lend or not to MFIs.

The Government and Reserve Bank of India are pushing the formal financial institutions to respond positively to FI needs, through opening fresh branches in un-banked regions, employing BCs to strengthen the last mile connectivity and helping to open no frill accounts. In terms of numbers progress may have appeared but actual benefits are not perceptible. Only a few accounts are activated. Though SHG outreach is over 95 millions, they are not included in the financial inclusion strategy of the government. This is denying opportunity to leverage and optimize the gains of a large programme. To accomplish financial inclusion for 600 millions un-banked people, convergence needs to be seriously deliberated. Due to the reluctance of main stream commercial banks to service poor women clients, the government has established a National Bank for Women. It is also exploring the possibility of establishing a new category of "Small Finance" Banks. All these policy initiatives will have impact over the times to come.

Strategy to Promote SHGs

New Initiatives

- Real development cannot take place unless poor people are mainstreamed into the banking system. Hence SHG program has to be institutionalized.
- Financial inclusion began with the SHG-Bank Linkage Program.
- Promote Farmer's Clubs through PACS.
- Use of IT platform for reaching out to the poor.
- With the Aadhar – enabled Kisan Credit cards, development of atleast one lakh SHGs in LWE districts.

Self Help Promoting Institutions (SHPIs)

The SHGs need Self Help Promoting Institutions (SHPIs) to promote and nurture them. The SHGPIs include Banks, Farmer's Clubs, government agencies, self employed individuals, SHG federations, NGOs.

Strategy

1. *Cooperative Banks to Function as SHPIs*

To accelerate the growth and spread of the program cooperative banks can function as SHPIs with need based grant assistance from NABARD. Each Cooperative bank can select initially, based on the selection parameters, upto 25–30 branches/PACS which would function as SHPI.

The cooperative banks already functioning as SHPIs, will also review their performance for expansion/scaling up their program.

2. *Enabling Provisions in Cooperative Societies Act/By-Laws & Rules*

Considering the obvious advantages of lending through SHGs, it is envisaged that Cooperative should have a significant role to play in making credit available to the rural poor through SHGs linkages. State Governments may consider making necessary enabling provisions through amendment in the respective Cooperative Societies Act/Bye-laws/Rules for bringing SHGs within the cooperative fold. The amendments made by many of the States like Kerala and Maharashtra, in the Cooperative Societies Act have enabled the SHGs to become members of PACS and avail loans.

Table 3.1: Grant Assistance to SHPIs for Promotion of SHGs under SHG-BLP in 2020–21

S. No.		*Physical*	*Financial*
1.	Grant Assistance sanctioned during 2020–21		0.54
2.	Cumulative sanctioned upto 31 March 2021		418.22
3.	Cumulative grant assistance sanctioned to anchor NGOs for promotion of SHGs under WSHG Development Scheme upto 31 March 2021		204.38
4.	Cumulative grant assistance sanctioned to JLGPIs for promotion of JLGs upto 31 March 2021		219.73

Source: Status of Micro Finance 2020–21, NABARD.

CHAPTER 4

Microfinance and Microenterprises

Learning Objectives

1. To understand the role of microenterprises in the economy
2. Relation between microfinance and microenterprise
3. Role of banks

Definition of Microenterprises

- Entrepreneurship and microenterprises have been recognized as factors that contribute to the economic development of a country. A microenterprise can essentially be defined as a small business with five or fewer employees. The term microenterprise is often used to a small business financed by microcredit. Similarly, when referring to a small, usually legal business that is not financed by microcredit, the term microbusiness (or microbusiness) is often used Internationally, most microenterprises are family businesses employing one or two persons. Microenterprise are those having a ceiling on investment in plant and machinery below Rs. 25 lakhs. For the service sector, the investment limits is Rs. 10 lakh.
- Most microenterprise owners are primarily interested in earning a living to support themselves and their families. Moreover micro enterprises specialize in providing goods or services for their local areas. Microenterprises serve a vital purpose in improving the quality of life for people in developing countries. Microfinance seeks to help microenterprises by loaning small amounts of capital to these businesses. This allows poor individuals or families to start their own businesses, earn income and benefit their communities.

  For example, a woman in a developing country may use microcredit to take out a loan and purchase a sewing machine. She could use the machine to establish a microenterprise that specializes in tailoring. The woman would increase her wealth and help her community by providing a service.

- Microenterprises (mE) are the smallest recognizable informal businesses; hardly distinguishable from the household, usually one person or family based. Small and medium enterprises (SME) occupy the space in between microenterprises and large corporations. With a regular turn over with investment of 25 lakhs to 5 crores; for service sector investment limit is 2 crores. SMEs are formally registered.
- Microenterprises have a significant role in the context of a) industrial backwardness, b) unemployment and c) scarcity of capital.
- Industrial backwardness, the following points highlight the five main reasons for the industrial backwardness of India. The reasons are:
  1. Social and Religious Institutions at the village level, society is rigidly divided into different castes even in the present socio cultural milieu.
  2. Shortage of Capital
  3. Shyness of Entrepreneurs
  4. Scarcity of Labour.
- Unemployment Government did not employ the technically trained Indians in its existing commercial and industrial undertakings. Because of industrial backwardness in these areas, there was scarcity of people resulting in shortage of skills. Though microenterprises is not a panacea for the complex problem of unemployment and poverty, yet their promotion is a viable and effective strategy for achieving gains in income and assets of the poor.
- Scarcity of capital in backward areas limited the growth of industries. Further, investment was discouraged by the absence of many profitable opportunities.
- Microenterprises contribute to the reduction of poverty and vulnerability of poor. It enables them to break the vicious cycle of poverty and enhance self-empowerment, respect and social dignity. It allows poor people to increase their income, accumulate assets, and enter into mainstream society. The benefits of starting micro-enterprises go beyond an individual and a household. Others in the society also get benefited from the microenterprise development as it fosters social relations or networks, civic engagement, community solidarity, and social capital.

Weak Infrastructure

- Backward countries lack an adequate and efficient means of transport and communications, a well-organized and developed banking system and adequate facilities for technical education. Without these no country can develop economically. Lack of adequate infrastructure is a big obstacle to economic growth.
- The constraints, particularly financial, that entrepreneurs face in establishing businesses in general and microenterprises especially, have a gender dimension. Women are more likely to be constrained than men in that they have on an average a smaller amount of capital for startup. Four reasons can be identified that work behind women's disadvantageous position in the capital market: (1) women are likely to have lesser amount of equity (2) They have less experience; (3) resource lenders, due to their outmoded gender beliefs may discriminate against women; and (4) the reduced rate of the number of applications for loans by women due to women's own belief that they will be discriminated (Carter *et al.*, 1997).
- The collateral requirement, finding a male guarantor for taking loans, the authorization of loan application by the husband or a male member in the household, preference of lenders for financing of those activities that are usually run by male, lack of knowledge about the availability of funding, discrimination, transaction costs, risk averse behavior of women and the literacy requirement are factors behind the gender discrimination in the financial sector.
- Considering the limitations of formal sector financial institutions in providing women with the amount of fund that is required for starting microenterprises; microcredit programs have evolved. Microcredit are small loans that are given to poor people without collateral for income generating purposes. Since the formal sector financial institutions, chiefly commercial banks, are male biased in terms of giving loans, microcredit programs target women for giving loans. The reason for women being targeted for microcredit loans is that women's access to credit has been recognized as an important factor that significantly contributes to the household welfare. The access of women to microcredit increases consumption, improves nutritional level, enhances aspiration for children's education in the household, and contributes to the reduction of household poverty. The main

objective of targeting women for giving microcredit is to empower women in the household through helping them to create self-employment for them by establishing microenterprises.

Bottom of Pyramid

It is called "the markets of those with the least".

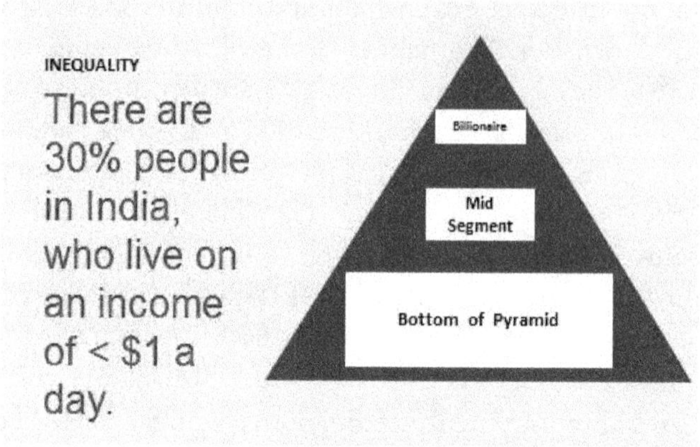

Fig. 4.1: Bottom of Pyramid

These are called "Bottom of the Pyramid" (BOP) markets. They are in excess of about four billion—of the world's poorest citizens. They constitute an invisible and unserved market blocked by challenging barriers. Thus, they are prevented from realizing their human potential for their own benefit. A member of the BOP is part of the largest but poorest groups of the world's population, who live with less than $2.50 a day. The base of the economic pyramid is by far the largest percent of the population and market in India. The estimates of BoP population in India range from 335 million to 1.05 billion people. On the low-end of the spectrum lies the official Government of India poverty line number, which assumes income of less than INR 32 per day in urban areas and INR 26 per day in rural areas and accounts for 30% of the total population. (This measurement has been publicly criticized for being unreasonably low). The McKinsey report states that as of 2005 1.05 billion people (or 5 out of 6 Indians) were BoP, living on an annual household income of less than INR 200,000 per year or 16,667 per month. While economic growth and innovative interventions are fueling some improvements and a growing middle class, the report projects that the BoP will still account for 78% of India's population or 997 million people by 2015.

- Rural people have limited access to resources or employment opportunities that would make them economically independent.

  MSME sector contributes 7.28% of GDP in the manufacturing Gross Output.

  In terms of Gross Output, microenterprises contribute 44.2% of the gross output of MSME sector, which is 312973 crores, in registered segment. In Unregistered segment, they contribute 87.87% of gross output (324873 crores).
- Microenterprises in India: Type of Ownership.

  In Microenterprises sector, majority of the ownership is proprietary. More than 90% of microenterprises are under proprietorship. This shows that majority of the microenterprises need extra support. Microenterprises contribute to the major share of employment generated in the MSME sector.
- Microenterprises are more attractive to them because it requires low capital and low risks.
- Microenterprises aim at the identification of innovative and creative activities.
- Suited to the specific environment in which people are living and
- Tries to solve the problem faced by the community by using technological know how
- Women also find microenterprises attractive because of low barriers to entry and the flexible nature of the work, which makes it easy to combine gainful... The high labour requirements of microenterprises can exclude poorer and more overworked women.

Role of Banks: Priority Sector Status for Bank Loans to MFIs

Banks need to become more involved with microenterprise through providing direct services and through support of microenterprises organizations that serve poor. Commercial banks need to undergo significant changes in their attitudes towards the poor. They need to change their structures and lending technologies if they are to play a major role in providing financial services to the poor. The RBI set up a committee to study issues and concerns in the microfinance sector (Chairman: Y.H. Malegam). Based on its recommendation, all SCBs were advised by the RBI that bank credit to MFIs should be extended on, or after April, 1 2011 for on-lending to individuals and also to members of SHGs/joint liability groups (JLGs). They were eligible for categorization as priority-sector advance under the categories agriculture, MSE, and micro credit (for other purposes), as indirect finance, provided not less than 85 percent of total assets of the MFI (other than cash balances with banks and financial institutions, government securities, and money market instruments) are in the nature of 'qualifying assets'. In addition, the aggregate amount of loan, extended for income-generating activity, should not be less than 75 percent of the total loans given by MFIs.

Graduation of Mature SHGs into Microenterprises

The banking system meets the core needs of savings and credit of SHGs. After these SHGs have availed loans from banks several times, they are now in a position to graduate into microenterprises by taking up income generating activities. Though identifying viable microenterprises is difficult, yet their promotion could be an effective strategy for achieving gains in income and assets of poor and marginalized people. In the absence of hand holding strategy to provide financial and non-financial services, graduation of SHG members from microfinance to microenterprises faced several obstacles.

Microenterprise Development Programme (MEDP) for Skill Development

MEDP was launched by NABARD in March 2006. The basic objective was to enhance the capacities of the members of matured SHGs to take up microenterprises through appropriate skill upgradation/development in the existing or new livelihood activities in farm and non-farm sectors. To enrich the knowledge of participants on enterprise management, business dynamics and rural markets, it was tailor-made and focused on skill building training programme. The duration of training programme ranged between 3 and 13 days depending upon the objective and nature of training.

The dominant activities in agriculture and allied sector covered under MEDPs were animal husbandry, bee-keeping, mushroom cultivation, vermicompost, organic manure, horticulture, floriculture, etc. Non-farm activities taken up under MEDPs were readymade garments, Agarbatti-making, embroidery, bamboo-craft, beauty parlours, etc.

Box 4.1: Women Led Entrepreneurship in Rural India

The last few years have seen interest among policy makers in women-led rural entrepreneurship. Much of it has sought to leverage the experience gathered from the estimated 45 million rural poor women mobilized through the Self Help Group (SHG) movement. These organizations, since their start in the 1990s have been an effective vehicle, especially in providing financial intermediation solutions for unbanked rural women.

India has, moreover witnessed state-led promotions of SHGs through a three tiered structure of community institutions at group, village, and cluster levels. These have been via both Central schemes—the Deendayal Antyodaya Yojana—National Rural livelihoods Mission for instance—and state government initiatives such as Kudambashree in Kerala and Jeevika in Bihar. There are today dedicated autonomous organizations—so—called State Rural Livelihoods Mission SRLMs—which even while bureaucrat—led, nurture SHG initiatives with the support of development sector professionals and last-mile community cadre. As the membership in SHGs has grown, there have also been attempts at thrusting new functions—including using them as a delivery channel for government projects, be it toilet construction (Swachh Bharat) or avenue tree plantations (the Haritha Haram scheme of Telangana).

All this, in a way, reflects a shift in the attitudes of the political class towards the SHG movement—from initial skepticism/suspicion of a potentially powerful parallel community structure, to welfare delivery and women's empowerment. But it would be naïve to say that these organizations have survived purely because of being co-opted by the politico-bureaucrat apparatus. Longevity of two decades is itself a good indicator of their resilience and, perhaps adaptability for a national scale development initiative.

The current policy intent is seemingly to reinvent the SHG movement with an economic development focus, emphasizing on women's entrepreneurship as an engine of growth in rural India. Notable examples of economic development initiatives through SHGs include the Café Kudumbashree chain of women-owned and operated canteens in Kerala and a maize producer company run by women in Bihar. Yet the shift in focus from community development to the hard metrics of a market also presents policy challenges of a different kind.

At present, SRLMs are the primary institution responsible for promoting entrepreneurship by SHGs. But these were vehicles built for social mobilization. An institution that seeks to promote an economic development agenda needs a different set of skill-sets. It probably calls for a new institution having a deep functional relationship with SLRMs, to leverage the latter's strengths of mobilization and last-mile presence. Such a state-level institution could even be a not—for profit company registered under Section 8 of the Companies Act 2012. We have the example here of the NDDB Dairy Services, which, modeled as a Section 8 company, has nurtured successful rural businesses and taken them to scale. This offers rich lessons that the new SHG-led economic development initiatives can learn from.

Second the internal management team of the proposed institution should be combination of young business management pro-department staff on deputation. Besides, state government must engage successful micro and small entrepreneurs as mentors to the new women SHG enterprises. This would mean a shift from the traditional approach of engaging only state agencies in microenterprise development initiatives.

Third, government financial support to the new promoting institution should be restricted to initial start-up costs, thus putting the onus on it to be lean in structure and generate own revenues to cover operating costs. The history of SRLMs is proof that the principle of autonomy mean nothing if these bodies are financially dependent on the state.

The government needs to realize that financial inclusion and economic development are two different functions, even if the target group is the same poor rural women. Social cohesion has been the binding factor for SHGs and vital to their success in financial intermediation. But economic development is a function where collectivization can work only if the business itself favours sharing of resources. And where business logic drives collectivization, the member—owned institutions should not blindly adopt, but adapt, the design principles of SHGs in terms of structure, culture, governance and management processes.

It is equally important to ensure that working on rural growth via SHGs should not end up in merely making women as instruments of change. In certain states, policy makers tasked with SHGs have targeted the household as a unit in economic development initiatives. This is based on a flawed assumption that livelihoods are a household function shared by men and women, whereas savings and credit are individual-led with women better positioned for that.

Rural microenterprises run by SHG members suffer from critical bottlenecks, whether in raising funds for start-up, growth and working capital or accessing high-quality technical assistance. Governments need to structure financial products addressing these needs, calling for a shift from a unit-cost based standardized budgeting approach. Evidence from the field should be used to improve access to collateral-free credit through institutions such as the Credit Guarantee Fund Trust for Micro and Small Enterprises. There is a tendency to club all microenterprises, including women-owned ones, into a singular category of subsistence-oriented outfits, i.e. those primarily run by households for own needs. Such categorization blunts customized support for those entrepreneurs needing specialized support to grow. States should adopt a pyramidal strategy for financial and technical assistance, based on the stage and size of enterprises. Lastly, the success of policy should not be measured based simply on the number of enterprises promoted and expenditures incurred. Amul's success today is read through both the 3.6 million milk producer-members in its network and an annual turnover exceeding $4 billion.

To conclude, the expansion in the SHG movement's scope, from social mobilization and financial inclusion objectives to economic development, is an organic step in the livelihoods chain. While this move from a producer to an entrepreneur is welcome, one mustn't lose sight of the fact that businesses are designed differently from savings groups or social units, and governments haven't proven their strength in promoting *dhanda* in rural areas. The business of entrepreneurship promotion is not the same as livelihoods promotion, as it requires treating SHG women as entrepreneurs and not just producers. Realizing this is key to achieving the twin goals of rural growth and promotion of women's entrepreneurship.

Support to Activity-based Groups

NABARD introduced a scheme for supporting small-scale activity based groups (ABGs) in 2008–09, wherein capacity building, production and investment credit and market-related support was extended. The scheme focused on forming and nurturing the groups engaged in similar economic activities, such as farmers, handloom weavers, craftsmen, fishermen, etc. to improve efficiency of their production and realize better terms from the market through economies of aggregation and scale. The scheme drew upon NABARD's existing modes of support and had both grant and loan components. While grant support covered expenditure on SHGs formation and training, extension services, establishing market linkages etc. bank loan/s covered investment activities and working capital needs of the SHGs. Banks were eligible to draw refinance for the loans provided in Activity-based Groups on the same terms as applicable for SHG's financing. In select cases, NABARD provided loans directly to registered SHGs or through the agencies promoting SHGs to establish few initial projects where none existed.

CHAPTER 5

Women Development through Income Generating Activities

Learning Objectives

1. Income Generating Activities (IGA)—Identification, promotion and development.
2. Group based Activity
3. Main Steps of the IGA Setting—Technical feasibility, Economic and Financial Profitability
4. Feasibility Study
5. Training and Capacity Building

Income Generating Activities (IGA)

The main thrust of women's development activities would be to assist women in the sustainable establishment of income generating activities to be undertaken in or near the home. This could be also one of the main objectives of the self-help female groups through its reinforcement of group promotion activities. IGAs tend to give women a higher status within the family and studies generally indicate that the greater the amount of income under women's control the greater amount devoted to their children's education health and nutrition. Generally incomes of women are used for the increase of the well being of the family. However it is essential to guarantee that women will have the control of the funds (saving funds loans etc.) and the free disposal of them to implement IGAs.

Identification of Income Generating Activities

- The identification of income generating activities should come from a bottom up approach. An IGA should correspond to the needs of women. The failure of this kind of project generally comes from a gap between identifying women's needs and designing viable project. This means that it may be implemented after some steps have been carried out.
- PRA with women to identify problems, elaboration of a negotiated development programme, group promotion. All these activities should be carried out using participatory methods.

In this context and according to the suggested strategy, it seems more appropriate to focus on planning, organizing and supporting IGAs than to give a list of activities.

Potential Income Generating Activities

- To the benefits for women, IGAs to be supported should be those traditionally undertaken by women, and located in or near the home.
- Potential IGAs should concern activities where women can use skills they already possess.
- Rural women have skills to do small-scale plant and agricultural and animal production, processing and preservation.
- Areas for potential promotion include home gardens (aromatic and medicinal plants and herbs vegetables), indoor plants, flowers, fruit tree nurseries, animal production dairy products, sewing, knitting embroidering, carpet making.
- Potentialities are various according, to the specific conditions of the village.
- Marketing must be carefully considered before undertaking any of these rural enterprises.
- Lack of marketing expertise is the major weakness of this kind of programme.

Food Drying Processing and Preservation

In many rural households women are seasonally involved with these activities.

They preserve surplus production for household consumption and for marketing when the family needs more cash.

However, the regular production of a standardized product for the market is still rare. Local products which could be produced are absent. Most notable of these are:

Dried Fruit, Vegetables and Herbs

- Vegetables such as tomatoes eggplants can be dried, as well as many fruit, such as figs, grapes, apricots and peaches.
- In Jordan the solar drying of fruit and vegetables is restricted to a few minor crops such as chilies, usually for household consumption.
- The market for these is as yet poorly developed but the world market is expanding every year.
- There is also a large market for edible and medicinal herbs which remains poorly supplied from local sources.

Processed Fruit and Vegetable

Production of jams, pickles, vegetable pastes, fruit juices could all increase farm income and women's income in particular since this would generally make use of existing skills and technology.

- Example of Women Entrepreneurs Association of Nepal (WEAN).

Packaging

Packaging is probably important in attracting consumers for local products when they must compete against imports.

Producers need advice about moving dried and processed products from rural areas to larger outlets in towns. The Federation of Jordanian Women carries out a project concerning herbs drying and packaging run at community level, with good results.

Marketing of Dairy Products

Preparation and Marketing of Dairy Products

Milk processing units be established in villages where there is a surplus of milk. Eg. Katraj, Gokul. Milk processing is one area of traditional female responsibility.

The knowledge of production techniques is already widespread in several families, in Jordan sheep milk products are generally preferred but locally goat products may be more popular. One of the main items that store well and is widely sold is jeemid (kind of dried yoghurt).

Agricultural Food Processing

Illustration Turmeric, chilli powders, tomato sauce made by Help of SHGs, Saswad.

As with agricultural food processing, the main needs are:

- to mobilize women
- to produce hygienic products of consistent quality and
- to match their output to local markets.

- A range of various products can be made: butter, ghee, cream, cheese, yoghurt, etc.
- They may be some possibility of reprocessing locally made cheese and packaging and marketing it through urban food stores where traditional local cheeses are not sold.
- This activity could be developed in livestock raising.

Agricultural Production

Some agricultural production activities can be carried out in order to provide income such as: vegetables, aromatic and medicinal plants flowers indoor plants and fruit tree nurseries.

- The market for aromatic and medicinal plants seems to be important. Vegetables and medicinal plants should be linked with processing and packaging activities.

  Different groups of women could implement these activities according to their own interests and skills, one specialized in production, the other in processing and packaging.
- Flowers and indoor plants production could interest villages located close to towns where there is a market for this kind of production. Eg. Hinjewadi near Pune.
- Fruit-tree nurseries could be established by women e.g. Wadi by BAIF. There is a market for high quality fruit-tree seedlings and a few women have competencies in this area. Biological produce (fruit and market garden produce) could be an interesting' alternative.

Livestock and Poultry Raising

Establishment and Improvement of Livestock and Poultry Raising

The first priority of many women (most of them belonging to the target group "low educational older women" is to establish or improve their animal production by buying cows, or improved poultry (particularly laying hen). Several NGOs support this activity in providing credit facilities and technical assistance, especially for sheep and Shami goats. IFAD projects which provide credit lines for livestock and poultry up grading. Of course this activity should be the object of caution especially for goat raising and considered according to the fodder availability and grazing land availability. However it is one of the most fitted to a category of women. Many, of them want to buy, only one cow, especially in remote villages.

- The implementation of livestock raising should be linked with improved forage production for efficient production of milk and meat.
- Furthermore it can allow at the same time fodder shrubs plantation in rangelands, what consequently should imply more involvement of women, in natural resources management.
- One of the principal constraints is the animal health problem which can happen. In that case poultry, which needs less investment, is less risky.

Agricultural and Animal Production

Other Activities Relevant to Agricultural and Animal Production

Mushroom Cultivation: It is already implemented at an experimental stage in a few households. Few women participate in the activity and seem to take more care and be more motivated. Training and extension for women is crucial. Moreover mushroom farmers could work in small self-help groups.

Silkworm Breeding: This activity, even if it has decreased these last years can provide income for women. Women are generally responsible for this activity.

At the present time the activity seems to take a new-interest according to the potential future market of sill; made carpet, General Women Union plans to establish a female silkworm breeders cooperative.

The interest of this activity is that it can provide small but stable income for poor households & be carried out at group level. Research is in progress to propose new mulberry tree varieties, more productive. Mulberry tree promotion in appropriate areas should not be underestimated and it could be relevant to go into thoroughly the possibility of silkworm breeding activity.

Beekeeping: Women in general do not show any spontaneous interest for beekeeping. Nevertheless it can be proposed to women.

- Forestry produce exploitation. Some fruits and cherries can be collected and sold to herbalist's shops.
- Laurus nobilis oil is used in soap making.

Handicrafts

- Support to develop handicrafts at village level is the priority request of young, especially carpet manufacturing, knitting and sewing. Eg wooden toys in Sindhudurg.

  These activities are traditional and integrated in the cultural context.
- Knitting and sewing development is firstly wanted to satisfy the household consumption. E.g. Manipur.

  Consequently, these activities are within competencies of social services (welfare societies, women's union, etc.).

Shopkeeper Activities

One of the main problems expressed is the lack of basic medical services. The possibilities to train one or few women in this field could be explored in order to establish a small people's dispensary at village level or at least a village pharmacy with basic medicines.

- The implementation creation of a bakery could be envisaged according to the supplying difficulties, linked to the setting up of improved ovens.

Micro and Small-Scale Enterprises

FAO Project support the setting up of micro and small-scale enterprises.

There is a gap between domestic handicrafts and those aiming at marketing, which needs business skills and of course entrepreneurship development will not be appropriate for all women. This aspect should be emphasized, in order to avoid the frustration of women who imagine that handicrafts are IGAs which are the easiest.

A viable strategy and would allow women to share their time between economically productive activities and domestic responsibilities. The final objective being to establish a sustainable women's group which would be able to manage and run its own small enterprise. The same strategy might be carried out for sewing and knitting.

Recommendations for Implementation

General Comments; Characteristics of IGAs

- *The* general tendency is for women to work in the home and produce goods for domestic consumption not for the market.
- However the aim of an IGA is:
  (a) To produce for the market and
  (b) Furthermore it can be called micro or small-scale enterprise, whether it is managed at individual or group level.
  (c) One of the main criteria to choose an IGA should be its profitability.
  (d) The emphasis must be on orientating them from the social welfare perspective and towards the provision of business development services.
- IGAs can be seen as the initiation phase in the progression to small business development. It is difficult to make the transition from being unemployed and lacking in skills to being self-employed and capable of managing a business operation.
- The first step is to acquire specific technical skills. Once women have this experience. The next step is to upgrade those skills and introduce women to basic business concepts and procedures.
- The transition from a social welfare to a micro and small enterprise approach is reflected by a market-driven approach.
- Not all women will have ability and potential to become entrepreneurs, and should be not forced to do so. However, those women who do show the interest and determination to make the move to self-employment should have access to training programs that will provide upgrading from technical skills to business skills.
- The progression would follow this course: unskilled worker—skilled worker—experienced worker-entrepreneur.

- IGAs should be in priority to those traditionally undertaken by women and located in or close to the house in order to be as far as possible accepted in the cultural context.
- As any innovation, the implementation of IGAs is going to modify the traditional context, since it means the increase of the economic—and consequently social—role of the woman at the household level.

Social Change

- It is obvious that a social change is a long process, generally, conditioned by economic imperatives. In a patriarchal structure of the family where men are decision makers in the household, there is no chance of success for the implementation of IGAs if they remain suspicious and not convinced of their interest for the family. Therefore it is essential during all steps of the IGA setting and especially from the beginning (identification and feasibility) to integrate males in the process.
- Awareness should be made to inform them about the advantages for the family (increase in living standards, incomes and food security).
- Resources for women represent resources for food security (experience has shown that resources in the hands of women often have a greater nutritional benefit to children than the same resources controlled by men and they are more likely than men to spend a given income on food for the family.
- Reducing gender disparities by enhancing the human and physical resources commanded by women leads to growth in household agricultural productivity, greater income and better food and nutrition security for all.
- Awareness with case studies in order to show the advantages of the IGA setting is essential to allay men's suspicions. At the beginning it is likely that only broad-minded men will accept the innovation, but good results should gradually decrease the resistance of the others and involve more and more households.

Group-Based Activities

- The same method, based on the awareness and the demonstration of the advantages should be implemented to raise the resistance of many women to group-based activities.

- Only economic advantages can be an incentive.
- Awareness should show that the best results at individual level can be obtained with group-based activities.
- Coopting should be the rule for the participation in group-based activities. Some women (generally single higher educated women) have spontaneously expressed the wish to start group activities.

Participation of Beneficiaries

- Target groups and participation of beneficiaries.
- Two target groups can be identified according to the skills: women who have already technical skills and those who have no specific skills but seem extremely motivated, generally young women with a good level of education.
- Determination of women will be the main criterion to develop an IGA.
- Group promotion will be encouraged for the implementation of IGAs which are more efficient to be run by several women.
- This does not mean that the production process must entirely be at group level (in many cases, such as animal production, individual production is much more efficient) and only one stage of the process can be run at group level, such as marketing.
- Young high-educated women will be more inter-active, since a lot of them have the wish to develop group-activities, like craft and food processing.
- Each IGA (individual or at group level) should be considered as a project and beneficiaries should take part in all stages of the project, from the identification to the implementation according to the bottom up approach above described.
- This is essential to reinforce the capacities and assure the self-reliance of the individuals or groups and in the same time allow the sustainability of the activity.

Main Steps of the IGA Setting

Identification

- The participants should ask themselves how they can obtain income from an activity, and identify the factors contributing to the success of IGAs.

- At the same time they should ask themselves if they are already involved in the activity. They need to be aware of these factors and to gauge their own skills when they consider embarking on an activity.
- Trainers or promoters should allow participants to express themselves freely and note all suggestions at this stage).

Technical Feasibility

- This involves finding out whether the women suggesting the activity have the required technical skills and, if not whether they can acquire them rapidly.
- The necessity of a minimum of professionalism should be emphasized to allow a minimum profitability of the activity.
- Good quality and competitive goods should be produced.
- Once the skills of each individual or group have been identified, other prerequisites for a technically feasible operation have to be established (for example water for home gardens, raw materials for handicrafts, feed for animal raising...)
- Management skills should not be forgotten since an IGA is an economic venture which needs specific skills in management.

Economic and Financial Profitability

- In addition to being technically feasible, the IGA should be profitable, that is to say they should produce income or a surplus (profit) and work without subsidies (sustainability).
- A profit-making activity should be profitable, in other words, returns should be higher than costs so as to produce a profit.
- Potential market should be identified and involved risks considered.

Feasibility Study

- The feasibility study is essential and should be conducted before starting any IGA (the results will allow to find out whether a proposed activity is a good idea or not!.
- The general socioeconomic context should not be ignored. On the contrary the IGAs should be integrated in this context especially for some activities (such village carpet unit).

Planning

Once the activity has been carefully chosen all the operations should be identified and listed in logical and chronological order.

- These operations should be scheduled and a timetable should be drawn up.
- This means that all facilities and resources needed to carry out a given operation must be available in good time to avoid delay and ensure that the other operations begin on schedule.
- All tasks should be planned in details.

Marketing

Plans for Marketing

- Products should be of good quality and competitive.
- Potential markets should be investigated.

Financing

Ways of Financing

- Since we are focusing, on profitable activities we should see the possibility of activities financed by the beneficiaries own funds and sources of potential forms of credit.
- It is difficult for most of women to support start-up costs by themselves due to the lack of savings.
- It is important that the real costs are supported by beneficiaries.
- Nevertheless an initial grant to cover start-up costs can help the establishment of the IGA in specific cases (high poverty for example).
- Grants and subsidies should carefully used because they distort the real costs and consequently the profitability of the IGA. In addition the can undermine the self-reliance of the beneficiaries.
- Credit may be distributed in several ways and different sources may be explored.
- Repaid loans guarantee the continuity of the project.
- Traditional banks give credit through normal channels providing the beneficiaries have guarantee.

- Promoting group loans (type Grameen Bank). It may be difficult to have small loans and individual borrowers can group their loans request together.
- The group loan will be granted with group liability. This means that each member is responsible for the other members of the group. If one member fails to repay her part others must repay it. This guarantees the repayment of the loan.

Group Promotion

- Emphasis should be made on IGA:
  - as a process to enhance capacities of women and
  - to promote and train sustainable self-help groups. As women may not be treated as passive recipients of assistance it is essential to build up their confidence in their own abilities and promoting their self reliance.
- To promote groups we can propose the following steps:
  - gather basic information
  - identify the living conditions of different socioeconomic groups in women's community
  - the power structure
  - the leaders (and potential leaders)
  - the existence of women's union members
  - identify women who are interested in working together and explain the objectives and interests of participator self-help groups (all members can benefit from their combined skills and resources);
  - explain the objectives
  - establish homogeneous groups formed around income generating activities on a voluntary and democratic basis and discuss goals and expectations.
  - establish an effective management structure with representatives: leaders, committees...
  - discuss the benefits of group income generating activities and present the IGA as a process with a number of steps and guide the members through the process; discuss problems, members' expectations and wishes;
  - discuss ideas for IGAs and help women decide which ideas are economically feasible;

- discuss the building blocks of the group activity to implement an IGA;
- conduct a feasibility study. Help the group to assess the skills of the members. The training needed and to study the market, the competition, resources needed, start up and operating costs, discuss the risks;
- reckon the profitability of the IGA;
- plan and schedule the steps to be implemented before launching the IGA and define commitments of the partners (Project, beneficiaries); emphasis should be made on vocational and management training;
- seek; and define the means of financing (credit, revolving fund in kind or in money, savings, etc.);
- launch the activity.

• The process of group formation will certainly face difficulties according to the fact there is no habit of this method and women are not accustomed to taking initiatives and decisions.

• Discuss the set objectives for the group, the work method (regular meetings, role of the members, leadership...).

Training and Capacity Building Needs

Beneficiaries

• Different types of awareness and training can be carried out according to the level of competencies of the potential beneficiaries:
  - awareness on the potential IGAs at village level. This awareness may be made after the women have identified some IGAs during participatory meetings.

• Some other IGAS, seeming appropriate to the characteristics of the village, may be presented. Basic information on the advantages and constraints, the main stages to be followed the types of possible organization;
  - training on the IGAs implementation process. Information on feasibility studies access to financial ways. financing methods (as revolving fund, savings...) management;
  - training on the management of revolving: fund;

- vocational training sessions relevant to various activities. The training programme should be established with the participation of beneficiaries.

- The courses can concern various matters (agricultural and animal production, food processing, handicrafts, etc.)
- Different kinds of courses can be carried out according to the level of competencies of women involved.
- A difference should be made between basic courses and reinforced courses which target skilled women.
- Some of these courses can be run at village level and specific courses should be made outside (rural centres, women's unions centres).

Small Scale Enterprises

- Training program on small scale enterprises. This program will target on women interested in creating small enterprises at individual or group level.
- It will focus on entrepreneurial development and management skills.
- The content should include specific areas such, as: management, organization, accounting, marketing, production techniques, quality control, cost benefit analysis, etc.)
- Entrepreneurship development training will not be appropriate for all women. This program will be designed to focus on those women who show entrepreneurial interest and drive, to tap that drive and combine entrepreneurial development with skills upgrading and training.

CHAPTER 6

Microfinance and Livelihoods

Learning Objectives

1. Definition of livelihood
2. Livelihood strategies
3. Microenterprise loans
4. Goals of livelihood promotion
5. Stages in Livelihood selection
6. Environment Analysis
7. Strategies in Livelihood promotion
8. Sustainable Livelihood and Microfinance

Definition of Livelihood

Livelihood is a way of keeping oneself meaningfully occupied, by using one's endowments (human and material), to generate adequate resources, to meet household requirements in a sustainable manner. Thus livelihood is not a one time job or work. Or earnings through lottery is not livelihood. It has to be over a period of time. Secondly livelihood is not limited by fixed time for example a 9–5 job. Further, one's endowments could be mental, physical (sportsman or an actor) Livelihood is significant to help people build upon their own strengths and realize their potential.

Doubling Farm Income for Sustainable Farming

India has a huge population, dependent on agriculture for livelihood. The growth of the larger economy depends on the economic potential of the agricultural sector. Hence the purchasing power of farmers is important. The growth rate for agriculture, forestry, and fishing sector slowed down to 1.7 per cent from 4.1% last year. Agriculture sector world over is vulnerable. Countries have tried various methodologies for supporting the sector. Some highly developed countries by different forms of subsidies have directly ensured that money goes into the pockets of the farmers and the countries that don't have that level of affordability have to struggle with the challenge that sustains level of farmer is maintained.

India is trying to double farmers income by 2020–22. Government has taken steps to improve upon rural infrastructure and at the same time to ensure that income is enhanced. The Government has taken various measure to improve rural infrastructure by building roads, electrifying villages, developing irrigation and providing regular dwellings. Credit availability interest subvention and crop insurance are other steps in that direction.

- Most rural households rely on multiple income sources. For example they may have income from agriculture, supplemented by dairy or poultry activities. They adopt a range of survival strategies. Migration to urban from rural areas or straddling that is some members stay in rural areas while others live semi permanently in urban areas. Now-a-days, as the population in urban areas is ageing, and because of nuclear families, there is no one to take care of the elderly. In the Home care sector, particularly young boys in their 20s, who would have otherwise worked on the farm; come to take care of the aged. This way they are supplementing the farm income. In case of need, for example if they have taken a loan from the money lender, they find this additional source of income handy.

Livelihood Strategies

- Livelihood from agriculture includes livestock rearing, aquaculture, forestry. Sometimes the farmer may combine different activities as a strategy to overcome natural disasters. For example, successful agricultural farming may include the Wadi Concept of BAIF by growing 2 to 3 crops and at the same time undertaking dairy or fish culture etc.
- Livelihood diversification may involve a wide income earning portfolio to cover all types of shocks jointly. It may involve focusing developing response to handle a particular type of stress to well develop coping mechanism. For example, the farmer can also a diversify into dairying, sericulture etc.

- Ownership rights of productive assets needs to be given to the poor; especially women. This is well illustrated in the case of village in Satara district (See Box 2.1 case study) Building assets in the hands of the poor ensures that financial institutions serving the poor need to place more emphasis on savings instruments. There is also the need for the introduction of social insurance such as insurance for health, child care and shelter.

Box 6.1: New Nameplates in Satara Have Both Mr & Mrs: Case Study

About 5,000 women in 20 villages of Satara district now own the home they live in. Another 500 are in the process of getting co-ownership of the family farmland as well. That's significant in a country where around 75% of rural women depend on agriculture for livelihood, yet just 12.78% own land according to the Agriculture census 2011. The impetus was a 2003 resolution passed by the Maharashtra rural development department called "Ghar Doghanche" or Home for Two. In effect, it means that the home should belong to both husband and wife. Little was done to ensure it was implemented. Until women were owners of the home and land that they worked so hard to till, they would continue to be an invisible labour force and victims of violence.

Increasingly land is being cultivated by women as men migrate to cities in search of work. Yet they remain the largest group of landless laborers. The idea that they could own their home was inspiring for women. It took time to convince men that they should include their wife's name in the marital home. Male fears and insecurities came up: would the women sell the property, desert her husband and take in another man?

Some men feared the women would go astray. Mobilizing women to ask for their 'hakk (right in Marathi) All married women in the village have homes in their names. Incidents of drunk men beating up wives have come down sharply since the ownership pattern changed.

Changes in India's land laws happened in 1980s. Five states—Kerala, Tamil Nadu, Maharashtra, Andhra and Karnatak—amended their laws between 1986 and 1994 to allow women to inherit agricultural land. Most recently the Hindu Succession (Amendment) act (HSAA) 2005 ruled that Hindu sons and daughters had equal rights to inherit agricultural land across all states, except Jammu and Kashmir.

Studies show that ownership of property acts as a catalyst to empower women to resist violence and encourages entrepreneurship and financial independence. Yet ground realities are different. Women hesitate to seek a share in parental property for fear of alienating their parents and siblings. In the marital home, assets are rarely transferred to women who seek property rights. Brutal murders & violence against women who seek property rights make headlines in urban India nearly every week. The Landesa study, which interviewed 1,436 women whose households had access to land, found that only 19% own land with documents that include their names. When researchers looked at how plots are registered, they found that women's names appeared in only 14% of the title deeds or documents.

Even in Satara villages, men have agreed to share home ownership, but are still reluctant to part with land rights. Men, however, say that land rights are ruled by 'parampara' or tradition. Although supportive of the move to give property rights to women-men feel that handing over land to women is inviting trouble.

It is a much longer process and ownership of land is very complex in India with fathers, brothers and other family members as stakeholders. But for now 5,000 women have become the true ardhanginis (or equal half) of their homes.

Ref: TOI, 12–11–2017, Pg.18.

Microenterprise Loans

- Grameen Bank provides larger loans called micro-enterprise loans for fast moving members. Power tiller, irrigation pumps, transport vehicle, river craft for transportation and fishing are popular items on which livelihoods are based and are supported by micro-enterprise loans. They help to increase the earning capacity of the member. There is no restriction on the loan size, but the repayment installments are pre-decided by the borrower.

Goals of Livelihood Promotion

- Creating assets of wealth It is important for farmers to build assets from income generating activities.
- Increasing food security. Food security is vital for the economic independence of the country.

- Reducing risk Mitigation of risk is important for the welfare of the farmers.
- Reducing variances in income one of the predicaments of the farmers is variances in income that farmers suffer due to seasonal variances or the changes in minimum support price (MSP).
- Reducing rural to urban migration Migration is a serious problem in villages as the young and able bodied move to urban cities in search of employment. To retain the people in villages it is important to create opportunities of livelihood in villages.
- Organizing producers to have greater control over their livelihoods, enhancing their money that circulates within the economy.

Stages in Livelihood Selection

- Identify various economic activities occurring in the rural areas.
- Extend a variety of technical assistance.
- Build up a network for input supply, marketing linkages etc.
- External support must be congruent with their existing livelihood strategies.
- And ability to adopt.

Environment Analysis

When identifying the livelihood activities, it is important to analyze the external and internal environment.

Strengths

Capabilities

1. The context in which (different groups of) rural people live. For example there may be a cluster of weavers or artisans whose skills are "paramparik" as they have been transferred over the generations.
2. The effects upon them of external trends (economic, technological, population growth, etc.), Economic trends like changes in the market economy, or technological trends like the use of Aadhar and IT enabled changes; similarly changes in the population whereby the population is becoming younger.
3. Shocks (whether natural or man-made) and seasonality.

External Environment

1. Their access to physical, human, financial, natural and social assets and their ability to put these to productive use.
2. The institutions, policies and organizations which shape their livelihoods.
3. The different strategies they adopt in pursuit of their goals.
4. Multiple-income sources.
5. Adopt a range of survival strategies (including various types of migration and straddling, whereby some members stay in rural areas while others live semi-permanently in urban areas).
6. Multiple actors (from the private sector to national-level ministries, from community-based organizations to the new decentralized government bodies), thereby widening the range of potential partners.
7. National and international linkages and the effect these have on people's livelihoods. Physical isolation of rural areas has led to the view that these linkages had little relevance.
8. They also stress the need for higher-level policy formulation to be based upon insights gained at the local level.

Sustainability

- In rural areas the sustainability of natural resources is important
- Vulnerability is a core dimension of poverty, hence people should be helped to develop resilience to external shocks and increase the sustainability of their livelihoods is therefore a priority.

Strategies in Livelihood Promotion

1. *Integrating Livelihoods:* The 'livelihoods approaches' work with people, supporting them to build upon their own strengths and realize their potential, while at the same time acknowledging the effects of policies and institutions, external shocks and trends
2. Identifying the constraints to livelihood development and poverty reduction. Such constraints can lie at the local level or in the broader economic and policy environment. They may relate to the agricultural sector or they may be more to do with social conditions, health, education or rural infrastructure.

Agricultural Intensification/Extension

- Livelihood from agriculture (including livestock rearing, aquaculture forestry, etc.)
- Through processes of intensification (more output per unit area through capital investment or increases in labour (inputs) or
- Extension (more land under cultivation).

Livelihood Diversification

- Diversify to a range of off-farm income-earning activities, or
- Migration
- Move away and seek a livelihood, either temporarily or permanently, elsewhere.

Sustainable Livelihood and Microfinance

- The sustainable livelihood is a result of strategy to scale up. If micro-finance or self help group continue to be limited to financial operations and does not extend to microenterprise initiatives growth will be a problem.
- This has been experienced by the Grameen Bank in Bangladesh and, since 2000 onwards, they offer micro-enterprise services as well.
- This helps an MFI in two ways,
  (a) ensures the sustainability of mF activities; and
  (b) ensures poverty reduction by providing employment and income to clients.
- The Millennium Development Goals declared by the United Nations to remove poverty should also serve to accelerate the introduction of a livelihoods approach to mF.

Weakness

- Vulnerability of livelihoods as it is affected by trend factors, shocks and seasonality.
- Access to credit cannot be seen as addressing their livelihoods concerns.
- The real manifestations of poverty are better captured by conditions of food insecurity and powerlessness and the empowerment issues.

Box 6.2: How Women's Business becomes that of Men

Despite the prevalence of small female entrepreneurs in developing countries, recent research suggests women do not benefit from loans and grants in same way that men do, leading to questions about the value of offering financial services to them. To measure the impact of credit and cash grant variations on microenterprise profits in households where women were the only entrepreneurs and in households where other members also had a business.

Easing financial constraints for female and male entrepreneurs in households with only one business led to comparable returns, but women attained lower return when multiple household members had their own business. This suggests that poor financial returns to female entrepreneurs did not indicate lack of ability, but rather that females' financial resources were often redirected to their husband's business.

In India, giving loan clients a grace period increased household—level business profits by around 45% but had no effect on female run business profits on average. This suggests that the average female client largely invested her loan in other household members' businesses; when the household had multiple entrepreneurs i.e. the female-operated business profits. But when a female client was the sole entrepreneur in her household, her business profits increased by around 75% relative to the standard contract.

Ref. IE: 13.12.2017

CHAPTER 7

Social Aspects of Microfinance

Learning Objectives

1. Microfinance: Minimalist approach and MF Plus Approach
2. Microfinance: Social and Economic Security
3. Savings
4. Insurance
5. Housing Loans
6. Other forms of security
7. Small Finance bank

Microfinance Minimal Approach and Microfinance Plus Approach

The question that arises is whether mF can be made to do more than just provide financial services on a small-scale? This brings out the distinction between minimalist mF-plus and mF-plus approaches.

- A Minimal approach is defined as the basic micro credit approach; where borrower's needs are limited to only micro credit or small loans.
- On the other hand, Micro-finance plus (mF plus approach) includes economic and business development services as well.
- Micro-finance plus plus includes, in addition, social services such as health and education including training and marketing assistance for microenterprises.
- In India, there is general agreement that mF should at least include the mF-plus component. However, issues about the ability of mF to adequately address livelihoods remain. To help in enterprise growth, especially by identifying opportunities, financial planning, and helping traditional manufacturing units respond to changing market demands.

- But at what level and how long such support, essential for the sustainability of the enterprise, should be there is not clear.

Microfinance Social and Economic Security

Empowerment

Poor people in addition to micro credit need access to financial services that include micro savings and insurance products, loans from emergency expenditure and basic assets such as housing and education. These services protect poor people from unforeseen crisis and emergencies in their households. It prevents them from following deeper into death trap and enable poor households to plan and manage their limited resources to meet their basic needs. As such the first step the poor people is social and economic security. Once, the poor households have greater security they are able to access microfinance products that help them develop their livelihoods. For the poor there may be little difference between savings, loans and insurance. Another factor for life cycle needs such as marriages, festivals and old age, emergencies such as illness, the death of a breadwinner and floods and investment opportunities Thus, Financial services not only take care of investment need of poor households but also address their security needs.

Savings

Savings are the first step to breakout of the vicious cycle of poverty. Savings can therefore be regarded as building assets and preparing the borrowers to take loans.

In the initial stages savings is vital. The people in informal sector are more than often trapped in a vicious cycle in poverty, because they have low income, they do not have capital to invest in assets to enhance their income. The income flows are small and not regular. Therefore, the primary need is to even out the cash flows by depositing part of the income in safe place which is accessible in times of need. Women in rural areas also need access to such product because of the seasonality of their income. It is important that poor learn to save as savings can contribute in following ways:

1. Enhance its member security
2. Savings building members capital for consumption, emergencies and investment

3. Protect them against borrowing from money lenders
4. They secure women's money by protecting it from their husbands
5. Reducing wasteful consumption
6. Instilling financial discipline
7. Give women a sense of security
8. Provide women with greater self esteem and giving their voice, recognition and status within their families.

The advantages of saving to the bank

Not only address the needs of its members to saving products but also there are significant advantages to the banks itself.

1. They provide a cheap and reliable source of fund.
2. Enhance their members micro business and hence their ability to absorb credit.
3. Reduce transaction cost on assessing potential borrowers.
4. Savings provide a good indicator of members ability to set aside part of their income for repayment.
5. To save regularly for some time before being eligible for loans.
6. Savings also reduce the risk on loans by acting as collateral.

Insurance

Poor households are vulnerable to events that are unplanned and beyond their control. A fire, theft, drought, flood or earthquake destroys their home and other assets that are means for their livelihoods. The poor are also vulnerable to loss of earning partly due to contingency within the family such as illness, death and pregnancy in case of women. Insurance provide security for the economic activities of poor rural producers. Insurance coverage for the poor in India is often unreliable and minuscule in scale and limited. Activities like farming do not have adequate risk cover. Similarly, in old age the farmers have no risk cover. Insurance services are an important part of microfinance. Insurance services not only help women to sustain financial shocks and reduce their losses but they also enable them to continue the process of building their assets and inculcate saving habits. They also help the bank in providing protection against defaults, caused by accidents or contingencies. The difficulties of insurance is that it is cumbersome in processing claims and mainstreaming companies providing coverage that is in appropriate or inadequate for the women and hence claims are rejected by the company. Another limitation is the lack of understanding among women themselves and their vulnerability to economic shocks.

Housing Loans

Women need flexible credit to sustain their micro business through periods of fluctuating income. Housing is another important security that women need. Housing loan enable women to build their portfolio of assets which can provide both income and security. Improving housing is way to provide better security and healthy living condition for the household by reducing the economic stress due to illness. The house also serves as loan collateral for the bank. Housing loan are used to improve an existing dwelling resulting in enhanced income stream from this activity. Housing loan help borrowers to build their portfolio of assets that can provide security as well as income. Housing loan provide visual evidence of the impact created by moving from thatched hut to a tile roof house provides a tangible result of the impact created. However, housing loan are possible only from third or fourth cycle of lending. Meaning that if a borrower has been with the organization for about three years. He or she has enough financial power to invest in housing creating additional outflows. However, evidence suggest housing loan is given less emphasis then saving and insurance.

Box 7.1: Triple Talak
Prof. Yunus has an interesting anecdote to share on housing loans to women. The Grameen Bank gives housing loans to women, which have become popular as it gives women security. Since the house is in the name of the woman, their husbands are afraid to say triple talak which would put them in a disadvantageous position.

Other Forms of Security

Another area of security for the family is education of children, particularly girl children. This attempts to shift attitude on girls education. In some villages in absence of schools girls have to walk long distances as a result there is high drop out rate. The government of Bihar decided to give bicycles to girls so that they could ride to the schools. Loans given by microfinance organizations are used primarily for paying tuition fees, purchase of books, uniform and another related expenses.

Housing is also important for self employed women who work from home. For these women investment in housing is as good as investment in their business because their home is their workplace, their workshop and their storehouse. Investment in housing safeguards their economic activities.

Apart from physical and economical need, there can also be the need for mental well being of a members. There can also be needs arising out of customs and social obligations. For example Sanghamithra an MFO promoted by the NGO MYRADA planned out an annual pilgrimage to Tirupati in Andhra Pradesh as this was an important need for which members wanted money.

Small Finance Bank

Box 7.2: Small Finance Bank

Navi Mumbai–headquartered microfinance institution (MFI) Suryoday is set to convert itself into a small finance bank. The company has been able to migrate its MFI operations to a banking platform using a cloud-based core banking platform provided by FIS.

R. Baskar Babu, founder CEO of Suryoday that the bank would start with 8 lakh borrowers who have availed microfinance loans. "The microfinance experience in Bangladesh has shown that small borrowers end up saving more than they borrow. Suryoday has a net worth of Rs. 350 crore.

Expanding Industry 9 Microfinance Cos that have Received Bank Licence	
• Bandhan* ! Kolkata • Disha Microfin ! Ahmedabad • Equitas Holdings* ! Chennai • ESAF Microfinance and Investments ! Chennai • Janalakshmi Financial Services ! Bengalure • RGVN (North East) Microfinance ! Guwahati	• Suryoday Microfinance ! Navi Mumbai • Ujjivan Financial Services ! Bengalure • Utkarsh Microfinance ! Varanasi

There are success stories like that of Pakistan's Tamer Bank which has built up deposits by operating post-midnight to cater to the fishing industry.

Ujjivan Small Finance Bank is expected to commence banking operations in the first quarter of 2017. Ujjivan Financial Services CEO and MD Samit Ghosh said, as a bank, it will now provide the full range of services to the un-banked and under—banked in the 24 states it operates in. "Our experience of functioning as an MFI (microfinance institution) for over a decade in the segments we have served will immensely benefit the future operations of Ujjivan Small Finance Bank.

For the quarter ended September 2017, Ujjivan reported nearly 90% increase in net profit to Rs. 73 crore, its gross loan book grew almost to Rs. 6,486 crore. It aims to give a personal touch. To continue with the personalized service, the company is in the process of hiring 1000 employees to reach to depositors.

Thus, micro financial services need to be much more widely available to the poor. While capacity building and technical assistance may be given to borrowers there may be some financial products that enable borrowers themselves to acquire education and skills.

CHAPTER 8

Role of ICT in Promotion of SHG and JLG

Learning Objectives

1. Advantages of IT
2. Criteria for technology, issues,
3. Use of smart phones-users gender wise
4. E-Shakti

Most poor people in developing countries still rely on physical delivery of cash to make payments or access financial services. This can be inconvenient and expensive for customers who may have to travel long hours to reach a bank or financial institution. It can also be expensive for financial service provider who don't have the infrastructure to serve customers in remote or rural areas. Mobile financial services provide a pathway to formal financial access in areas that physical banks cannot reach.

New financial service delivery models are emerging that leverage technology to deliver financial services in faster, cheaper and more convenient ways. The number of unique mobile subscribers has grown dramatically in the last decade and now more than 10 billion mobile connections are existing globally, and four out of five connections are in the developing world. New technology takes advantages of this mobile prevalence to make financial transactions more accessible and reliable. In many countries such as Kenya, a persons mobile phone is now in essence their bank account. M-PESA, a service that allows for money transfers via a cell phone, is probably the most well-known application of mobile technology for financial services. Over two-thirds of Kenya's adult population now uses the service to pay for every day expenses, such as taxis, utility bills or even individuals purchases. M-PESA originated in Kenya, but as of July 2014, there were 246 additional mobile money services worldwide.

- Technology is a successful way to improve the existing system into smaller forms. Through technology we are able to save money, energy and time in transferring social security pension, food money, MNREGA wages and so many others government sponsored benefits through DBT schemes. However, it hardly made minimal impact or dent on poverty. There is a need to expand Scientific Technology for sustainable economic growth in small increments. Technology always helped us in solving problems related to production of goods economically and in reshaping new kinds of products and services to fulfill the demands of the society. We need to develop and incorporate technological solutions in the field of agriculture and food processing. There is a huge demand for organic products in the urban society. They look for organic foods, free from pesticides, fertilizers and intoxicant sprays. There is a need to encourage such small industrial units for processing and preserving nutrients. Producers need to be trained and through use of technology, technical training could be provided at people's door step.
- IT has made significant contribution in the transfer of money and knowledge of financial products. The PMJDY has used technology for wider reach. This is the first step of the journey from poverty to wealth. However, 80 percent of the accounts opened under the scheme have zero balance. Many might have opened multiple accounts to get benefits under the government schemes after it was Aadhar-linked. The role of technology based solutions in leapfrogging barriers of remoteness and literacy has been widely acknowledged. In India, the credo of "JAM"—Jan Dhan, Aadhar and Mobile, aptly sums this up. It remains to be seen, however, if JAM is being implemented in the right spirit and with appropriate linkages to livelihood promotion and economic empowerment.

Information Technology—Advantages

- Transforming data into information essentially to aid the management

- Manage efficiently for decision making
- Expanded and inexpensive capacity of storage
- Increasing speed processing of data
- Different options of electronic devices to communicate with each other
- Identify electronic data management needs
- Identify IT solutions that will fulfill organization's information needs for organization's growth.

Criteria for Technology

1. Easily useable
2. Serve business
3. Cost effective

Mobile Devices

- Computers with smaller chips.
- Integration of IT systems with mobile devices.
- Invest in proven and robust mobile based devices that can improve operations.
- New technology refers to application of mobile devices in Micro-finance.

Issues

- Sometimes records are scanty or data that is never used
- WANTS to generate—which records are generated?
- Identify the records that come out of these.
- WHAT to do with it
  - optimization of records
  - relevance of information
- HOW it generates.

Necessary Information

Important information for loan officer is what repayments are due? Then it is important for them to organize recovery. In case of branch officers-productivity of their loan officers *vis-a-vis* productivity of other branches/ MFIs. Data collected should serve these needs.

IT Application Contribution

- Cost reduction
- Quality management
- Scaling up
- Improve ROI
- IT Applications and MIS: Sector Perspective
- Consolidating performance data will enable each of them to benchmark themselves against their peers.
- Thus improve senior management decision making.
- Sharing risk data will help all MFIs to manage their risk better.
- Sharing performance and product data will raise the understanding of the wider public and thus generate trust:
    - which translate into increased demand,
    - investment inflows and
    - into a more favorable regulatory environment
- Examples of Industry Wide IT Applications
- Data exchange facility to enable interaction between MFIs and also other stakeholders like insurance companies, banks, etc.
- A national MF data base to consolidate performance data.
- A credit bureau.

Smart Phones and Rural Women—Some Examples

- In Western Uttar Pradesh, Telenor has helped provide livelihood opportunities to local women who work as promoters and brought over 75,000 rural subscribers into the mobile net work. Smartphones are helping rural women get better at business across sectors.
- In Kotagiri in the Nilgiris, women self help group members are using social media to market their chocolates, pastries, tea and spicy goody bags in urban centres.
- Self Employed Women's Association (SEWA) has developed a mobile app for rural women entrepreneurs to sell farm produce like pulses, wheat and turmeric. Women place orders real time, record sales and maintain sales report and customers ledgers.

Application of IT: Urban and Rural Divide, Genderwise

- As the figure below shows, among only 38% are females in urban areas and an equal number are using internet. This shows that about 1/3rd females are net savvy.
- Rural women are less mobile savvy than their urban counterparts. In rural India, male to female internet use is skewed at 88:12 as compared to 62:38 in urban India.
- Internet penetration among rural females is growing at 61% and 79% among males.
- Internet use in rural areas is largely with mobiles and not much with laptops, PCs, tablets and other devices.
- In the rural areas, the number of female users are still less. There are only 12% women using the net in rural areas. There is a large potential for women in rural areas to use the net. If the reasons behind their restrictions imposed by village sabhas are removed, women will start using the net in greater numbers.

209 Million Urban Indians	*Are Using Internet*	*108 Millions Rural Indians Use Internet*	*Are Using Internet*
62% urban users are male	38% urban users are female	88% rural users are male	12% rural users are female
Still a Long Way to Go...			

Fig. 3: Urban and Rural Users Gender Wise

Factors for Less IT Usage

- For nearly a decade, social dogma has restricted women's access to mobile telephony. In some parts, Khaps have issued decrees barring unmarried women from owning cell phones, seen as a symbol of promiscuity.
- Women in India are 36% less likely to own a mobile than men.
- The findings show that lack of address and ID proof among women, particularly migrant workers is one of the many reasons they do not own mobiles.
- Cost is also a barrier because many are financially dependent on male earning members of the household, and often have to borrow handsets.

- Lack of education and familiarity with English has prevented mobile phones from reaching the last mile in the female segment.
- However more hand set makers are coming up with local language enabled handsets.
- In 2014, Telenor India study in UP's Aligarh district, a majority of men were found to have smartphones, while women made do with basic phones.
- While we associate mobiles with progress, a patriarchal mindset often associates cell phones in the hands of women with "evils" in society.
- Telenor has been working to bridge this gap through street plays and door to door contacts with families, female promoters explain the benefit of mobile connectivity to people.
- In Western Uttar Pradesh, Telenor has helped provide livelihood opportunities to local women who work as promoters and brought over 75,000 rural subscribers into the mobile net work.

Pradhan Mantri Jan Dhan Yojana

The Pradhan Mantri Jan Dhan Yojana, the government's flagship social welfare programme was to ensuring every family in the country at least one bank account. The Jan Dhan Yojana provides for a free zero-balance account with a debit card, Rs. 1 lakh accidental insurance policy and Rs. 30,000 free medical insurance cover Use of IT platform for reaching out to the poor. The account can be opened with Aadhar Card in any public sector bank or special camp held for the purpose. Each accounts comes with a RuPay debit card.

EShakti

EShakti or Digitisation of SHGs is an initiative of Micro Credit and Innovations Department of NABARD. In line with the statement of the Hon'ble PM 'we move with the dream of electronic digital India...'. Digital India is a Rs. 1.13 lakh crore initiative of Government of India to integrate the government departments and the people of India to ensure effective governance. It is to "transform India into digital empowered society and knowledge economy". Keeping in view the Government of India's mission for creating a digital India, NABARD launched a project for digitisation of all Self Help Group (SHG) in the country. The project is being implemented in 100 districts across the country.

Aims and Objectives

The project aims at:

(a) Digitization of all the SHG accounts.
(b) To bring SHG members under the fold of Financial Inclusion thereby helping them access wider range of financial services and
(c) To increase the bankers' comfort in credit appraisal and linkage by way of:
  - Integrating SHG members with the national Financial Inclusion agenda;
  - Improving the quality of interface between SHG members and Banks for efficient and hassle free delivery of banking services by using the available technology;
  - Facilitate convergence of delivery system with SHGs using Aadhaar linked identity.

The Background

The need of digitization of records of SHGs was felt due to delay in maintenance of books of accounts. Transparent and proper maintenance of records of SHGs facilitated nurturing and strengthening of SHGs.

It was also felt that digital empowerment will help in bringing SHGs on a common web based e-platform by making book keeping easy for low literacy clients. This would help in promoting national agenda of Financial Inclusion. Secondly it would pave the way of credibility of SHG data which can be used by Credit Bureaus to reduce the issues related to multiple financing by banks.

Stakeholders of the Project

Rural poor community and members of SHGs, Self Help Promoting Institutions (SHPI), Non-Government Organisations (NGOs), Banks, NABARD, Government development departments and agencies like SLRM, NLRM etc. At a later stage Credit Bureaus may also be on board.

Attributes of the Project

- E-book keeping for the SHGs.
- Regular updates of transactional data.
- Reports generated in the formats as required by stakeholders like bankers.

- Inbuilt automatic grading of SHGs based on NABARD/IBA (for NRLM) norms.
- Auto generation of Loan application for the bankers on input of resolution to borrow by SHG.

The project will also helps in:

- A comprehensive information base and robust MIS about poor community covered.
- This will facilitate suitable interventions and convergence of other programme for social and financial empowerment.
- It will help in identifying suitable interventions and support for proper nurturing and strengthening of SHGs.
- Ease of transfer of social benefits and Direct Benefit Transfer (DBT) through Aadhaar linked accounts and convergence with other Government benefits.

The USP of EShakti software is 'one-click' availability of social and financial information of all the members of the Self Help Groups.

Components of the Project

- Mapping of the existing SHGs in the district (bank wise, branch wise).
- Training of volunteers to collect SHG wise/member wise data.
- Data feeding through a customized software in central server.
- Hosting of data on the web under a dedicated website
- i.e. www.eshakti.nabard.org.
- Maintaining data center and data recovery center.
- Regular update of the transactional data.
- Generating MIS for various users.

Process

Information of all the SHGs and their members are uploaded onto the website. The transactions are updated through 'apps' on android Mobile/Tablet. Data authenticity is ensured through SMS alerts to members and sample audits. MIS reports on groups are generated and progress is tracked on a real time basis. Overall, the whole ecosystem was designed to address the complex issue related to patchy financial records of SHGs.

Information Captured

@Member Level

Name, address, gender, marital status, Physically Challenge status, Aadhaar details, Voter ID card details, mobile number, BPL/APL status, membership of any Joint Liability Group (JLG), house type, availability of toilets, electricity connection and other financial details like saving bank account number, savings, borrowing & repayment, life/medical insurance, micro pension policy (if any).

@SHG Level

Name, address, date of formation, name of SHPI/NGO, programme under which supported, savings habits, lending policy, bank linkage, details of periodic savings collected and internal lending, utilization of bank credit availed for members.

Output and MIS

- Member wise details of SHGs on saving, lending, attendance.
- SHG and member wise credit history.
- Financial statement of SHGs—Balance sheet and Profit and Loss account.
- Grading chart of SHGs.
- Micro Credit Plan of the SHGs.
- Audit report.
- Bank linkage details—savings and credit disbursement.
- Other periodical MIS on performance of SHGs.

Impact

- Provided credit to SHGs based on real time performance.
- Significantly reduced Saving-Credit linkage gap.
- Captured credit history of members.
- Promoted transparency through real time SMS alerts in 10 languages to members.
- Aided convergence of SHGs with other Government Programmes.
- Integrated members with the larger Financial Inclusion Agenda.

Paving way for Credit Linkage

- Bank branches to access the portal through Intranet or web link using their branch IFSC and password.
- More than 31 MIS reports like Savings, meeting, Credit linkage, Repayment and Demand Collection Balance can be generated from the Bank branch itself.
- Easier processing of loan using EShakti system generated prefilled application forms with all the members and group information.

Challenges

- Sourcing of information from poor database and records.
- Large scale training and capacity building of SHGs, SHPIs and others involved in implementation of the programme.
- Capture of field level information from SHGs in a limited time and periodic upload of savings and credit details of SHGs.
- Cooperation from banks.
- GPRS connectivity.
- Initial funding of the pilot is being met by NABARD. There will be a huge fund requirement for scaling this pilot from the present level to 86 lakh SHGs across the country.

CHAPTER 9

Joint Liability Groups

Learning Objectives

1. To understand the concept and features of JLG
2. To appreciate difference between SHG and JLG
3. To know the extent of financing of JLGs in the country

In 2004–05, Nabard started a pilot project on Joint Liability Groups (JLGs) The Grameen model is a form of JLG. JLGs are of 5 members. JLG comprises of groups of individuals who come together to borrow from the financial institutions. They share "responsibility" and stand as guarantee for each other. There is a group leader. Such groups are popular in urban areas as it helps in "financial inclusion".

Features

- JLG members offer a joint undertaking to the bank that enables them to avail loans.
- The JLG members are expected to engage in similar type of economic activities like crop production.
- The management of the JLG is to be kept simple with little or no financial administration within the group.
- JLGs can be formed primarily consisting of tenant farmers and small farmers cultivating land without possessing proper title of their land/ rural entrepreneurs engaged in non-farm activities.

Credit Assessment

- The JLG prepares a credit plan for its individual members and an aggregate of that is submitted to the banks. Banks may evolve simple loan application for this purpose.
- The individual members of JLG would be eligible for bank loan after the bank verifies the individual members' credentials.

Purposes of Credit

- The finance to JLG is expected to be a flexible credit product addressing the credit requirements of its members including crop production, consumption, marketing and other productive purposes.
- Banks may consider cash credit, short-term loan or term loan depending upon the purpose of loan.

Grameen Model

The JLG concept is based on the Grameen model. The highlights of the Grameen Model are:

- Banking without collateral.
- Generosity of heart and empathy.
- High priority to women.
- No legal instrument.
- Institutional set up.

JLG Models

JLGs can be financed by banks by adopting anyone of the following two models.

Individual Methods; Financing Individuals in the Group

The group is eligible for assessing separate individual loans from the financing bank. All members jointly execute one inter-se document; making each one jointly and severally liable for repayment of all loans taken by all individuals in the group. The financing bank assesses the credit requirement depending on the activities being undertaken and credit absorption capacity of the individual. Loans are provided to individuals based on his/her creditworthiness. If they need bigger loans, they are given based on their capacity to produce guarantee from friends and relatives. They comprise of lower middle class segment of clients. Loans are given primarily for business purpose. There has to be mutual agreement and consensus among all members about the amount of individual debt liability. Documents to be obtained include introduction form, application cum appraisal form and mutual guarantee.

Financing the Group

The JLG consisting of 4–10 individuals functions as one borrowing unit. The group is eligible for assessing one loan, which is combined credit requirement of all it's members. For example, in case of crop loan, the credit assessment of the group would be based on crop/s to be grown and the available area cultivable by each member of the JLG. All members jointly execute the document and own the debt liability jointly and severally. Documents as applicable to SHGs are adopted.

Table 9.1: Difference between SHG & JLG

Sr. No.	*SHGs*	*JLG*
1.	• Savings is important	• No element of savings
2.	• 6 to 12 months before loan from banks • Internal lending	• No gestation period • Loaning may take place once the group is formed
3.	• Accounts maintained by group	• No need of maintaining accounts by the group
4.	• Regular group meeting	• No regular group meeting
5.	• Quantum of loan is decided by group	• Quantum decided individually

Types of Loan

Banks consider cash credit, short term loan or composite loan (working capital with term loan) depending upon the purpose of loan. It is important that no collateral is insisted by the banks against their loans to JLGs. However, mutual guarantees as offered by the JLG members is kept on record. RBI may apply margins as per prescribed norms.

JLGs in India

Financing of Joint Liability Groups

- Financing to JLGs is part of priority sector lending. Banks may include JLGs in their business plan and training schedule. Financing of JLGs on the basis of studies conducted by NABARD, was found to be a good business propositions. It needed simplified documentation, group dynamics, timely repayment and prospects of credit enhancements to good clients. Comprehensive guidelines on JLGs has been issued to banks to focus on small and marginal farmers, oral lassies, tenant farmers and other clients under non-farm activities. NABARD supports bank for nurturing and financing of JLGs for the initial three years, Banks may also use the services of JLG promoting institution.
- NABARD has been popularizing the scheme and detailed guidelines for financing of JLGs was issued to all banks. Apart from extending 100% refinance support to Banks, NABARD extended financial stakeholders of this programme. Besides, NABARD extended grant support for formation and nurturing of JLGs to banks and other JLG promoting agencies. The Southern States topped the list with over 8.01 lakh JLGs organized so far, Eastern Region followed closely with 7 lakh JLGs. In terms of loans disbursed, however, Southern States accounted for nearly 41% of the total loans disbursed. With a view to sensitising the stakeholders of the JLG programme, NABARD arranged training programmes and exposure visits to successful JLGs, to the functionaries of these institutions including financing banks.

Table 9.2: Data on Joint Liability Group

		Physical	*Financial*
I	Joint Liability Group promoted during the year 2020–21	41.27	
II	Loan disbursed to Joint Liability Groups (JLGs) during 2020–21		58,311.78
III	Cumulative Joint Liability Groups promoted and loans outstanding as on 31 March, 2021	133.83	213,164.87

Source: Status of Micro Finance, 2020–21, NABARD.

Region-wise no. of JLGs promoted as on 31 March 2021 (in lakhs)

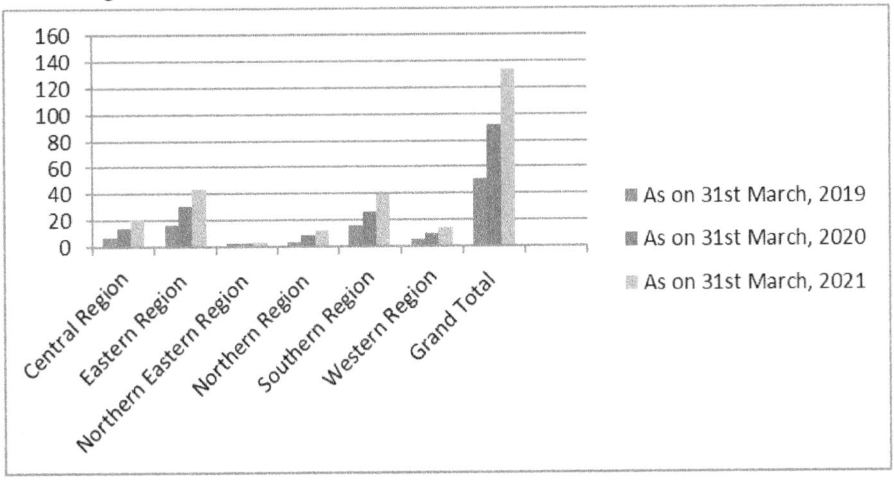

Fig. 9.1:

	Central Region	*Eastern Region*	*Northern Eastern Region*	*Northern Region*	*Southern Region*	*Western Region*	*Grand Total*
As on 31st March, 2019	6.72	16.9	2.18	3.74	15.72	5.5	50.76
As on 31st March, 2020	13.64	31.01	2.19	8.36	26.62	10.01	91.83
As on 31st March, 2021	21.3	43.47	3.29	12.48	39.35	13.94	133.83

Source: Status of Microfinance in India 2020–21, NABARD.

Grants Support for JLGs

To facilitate promotion of JLGs, NABARD provided grant assistance to banks and other institutions involved in promotion and nurturing of JLGs. JLG promoting institute is expected to formulate a plan for a minimum of 20 JLGs. Grant assistance of Rs. 2,000 per JLG is extended to banks for formation, nurturing and financing of JLGs over a period of three years. The first installment of Rs. 1,000 is released to the Bank/other institutions after sanction of loan by the bank. The second installment is released after commencement of repayment. The third installment is released in third year subject co certification of bank with regard to satisfactory repayment.

Summary

The global financial melt down has given an opportunity to create a financial system that is more inclusive Social business which combine altruism with business models to bring corporate efficiency and innovation to help the poor.

CHAPTER 10

Financial Inclusion

Learning Objectives

1. Need for financial inclusion
2. Role of financial inclusion in economic development
3. Financial inclusion in India

"Financial inclusion is a key determinant of sustainable and inclusive growth, which in turn is essential for building an equitable society."

Pranab Mukherjee, President of India

Of the 2.5 billion adults, just over half of world's adult population, do not use formal financial services to save or borrow; about 2.2 billion of these un-served adults live in Africa, Asia, Latin America, and the Middle East. Of the 1.2 billion adults who use formal financial services in Africa, Asia, and the Middle East, at least two-thirds, a little more than 800 million, live on less than $5 per day (McKinsey & Company, 2009). In India, for 6.34 lakh villages, 44,699 bank branches exist and the total no. of bank branches for the country as a whole as of March 2014 was 1,16,450. On an average, 5000 branches are added per annum. Out of 24.67 crore households in the country, only about 14.48 crore or 58.70 per cent households had access to banking services (Govt. of India, 2011). Thus, a large segment of society, particularly low income people, have very little access to financial services, either formal or semi-formal. Consequently, many of them have to depend either on their own or on high cost informal sources of finance, such as the money lender.

According to a United Nations report, financial inclusion encompasses two dimensions of customer access. First, it refers to a customer with access to a range of formal financial services, from simple ones like credit and savings to more complex ones like insurance and pensions. Second, it implies that customers have access to more United Nations (2006), Building inclusive financial sectors for development, New York than one provider of financial services, thus, increasing access to a variety of competitive options.

According to Usha Throat financial inclusion is important to India for the reasons as given below:

> Limited access to affordable financial services such as savings, loan, remittance and insurance services by the vast majority of the population in the rural areas and unorganized sector is believed to be acting as a constraint to the growth impetus.

Access to affordable financial services, especially, credit and insurance, enlarges livelihood opportunities and empowers the poor to take charge of their lives. Such empowerment aids social and political stability. Apart from these benefits, financial inclusion imparts formal identity, provides access to the payments system and to savings safety net like deposit insurance.

Hence financial inclusion is considered to be critical for achieving inclusive growth; which itself is required for ensuring overall sustainable growth in the country.

In recent years 'Financial inclusion' has been on the policy agenda of many developing countries. Policy makers and central bankers from around the world came together in different forums to discuss,' Financial Inclusion' and to build financially inclusive economy. An Inclusive financial system implies availability of a continuum of financial services for all income groups and a wide range of financial services with no gaps in provision. Further Financial inclusion does not imply that everyone will use all available financial services but rather they have an option to use them.

Role of Financial Inclusion in Economic Development

Financial inclusion is critical as increasing the poor's access to financial services is often considered as an effective tool that can help reduce poverty and lower income inequality.

Thorat, U. (2007), Financial Inclusion—The Indian experience. Speech presented at the HMT-DFID Financial Inclusion Conference 2007, Whitehall Place, London, UK.

Financial inclusion is a broad concept. As defined by Sarma (2008), financial inclusion is the process that ensures the ease of access, availability, and usage of formal financial system for all members of an economy. Financial Inclusion will enable to achieve following objectives:

1. ***Economic Objectives:*** For the equitable growth in all the sections of the society leading to a reduction of disparities in terms of income and savings the financial inclusion can serve as a boom for the underdeveloped and developing nations.
2. ***Mobilization of Savings:*** If the weaker sections are provided with the facility of banking services the savings can be mobilized and can be effectively utilized for the capital formation and growth of the economy.
3. ***Larger Market for the Financial System:*** To serve the requirements and need of the large section of society there is an urgent need for the larger market for the financial system; to open up the avenue for the new players in the financial sector and lead to growth of banking sector.
4. ***Social Objectives:*** Poverty Eradication is considered to be the main sole objective of the financial inclusion scheme since they bridge the gap between the weaker section of society and the sources of livelihood and the means of income which can be generated for them if they get loans and advances.
5. ***Sustainable Livelihood:*** Once the weaker section of society got some money in loan form they can start up their own business or they can support their education through which they can sustain their livelihood. Thus financial inclusion has turned out to be a boon for the low income households.
6. ***Political Objectives:*** There are certain other political objectives which can be achieved with the wider inclusion of lower strata in the society and an effective direction can be given to the government program.

Conceptual Issues and Relevance of Financial Inclusion

Meaning of Financial Inclusion

Many authors, economists, researchers, policy makers, institutions etc., have defined Financial Inclusion. A few definitions on Financial Inclusion are presented as follows:

Definitions

Asian Development Bank (2000) "Financial Inclusion is the process of ensuring access to appropriate financial products and services—deposit accounts, payment services, micro-credit and micro-level insurance—to vulnerable groups such as weaker sections and low income groups by mainstream institutional players."

- *Rangarajan Committee (2008):* Financial inclusion may be defined as the process of ensuring access to financial services and timely and adequate credit where needed by vulnerable groups such as weaker sections and low income groups at an affordable cost.
- *RBI's Definition:* Financial Inclusion is the process of ensuring access to appropriate financial products and services needed by all sections of the society in general and vulnerable groups such as weaker sections and low income groups in particular at an affordable cost in a fair and transparent manner by mainstream institutional players.
- *Raghuram Rajan Committee:* Financial inclusion, broadly defined, refers to universal access to a wide range of financial services at a reasonable cost. These include not only banking products but also other financial services such as insurance and equity products.
- *Treasury Committee, House of Commons, UK (2004)*, "Ability of individuals to access appropriate financial products and services".
- *United Nations (2006)* financial sector that provides access to credit for all bankable' people and firms, to insurance for all insurable people and firms and to savings and payments services for everyone. Inclusive finance does not require that everyone who is eligible use each of the services but they should be able to choose to use them if desired.
- *Claessens (2006)* has defined financial inclusion as the "availability of a supply of reasonable quality financial services at reasonable costs, where reasonable quality and reasonable cost have to be defined

relative to some objective standard, with costs reflecting all pecuniary and non-pecuniary cost."

- *CGAP:* Financial Inclusion may be defined as the process of ensuring access to financial services and adequate credit when needed by vulnerable group such as weaker section and low income group at an affordable cost.
- *G20:* Financial Inclusion refers to a state in which all working age adults have effective access to credit, savings, payment, and insurance from formal service providers. "Effective access" involves convenient and responsible service delivery, at a cost affordable to the customer and sustainable for the provider, with the result that financially excluded customers use formal financial services rather than existing informal options
- ***Dr. K.C. Chakrabarty, Deputy Governor RBI (2011)*** states "Financial inclusion is the process of ensuring access to appropriate financial products and services needed by all sections of the society in general and vulnerable groups such as weaker sections and low income groups in particular at an affordable cost in a fair and transparent manner by main stream institutional players".

  Alfred Hannig, "Financial inclusion is no longer a side issue in the global economic debate. It now has a permanent and important place in the global discussion on economic development and stability."

  S. Claessens, 'Access to Financial services. A review of the Issues and Punlic Policy Objectives,' the World Bank Research Observier, Vol. 21, No. 2, 2006, pp. 207–240.
- ***Crisil Inclusix,*** "Financial inclusion... is not just about opening of saving bank accounts; it includes creation of awareness about financial products, and offering of advice on money management and debt counseling."
- ***Rangarajan Committee,*** "financial inclusion may be defined as the process of ensuring access to financial services and timely and adequate credit where needed by vulnerable groups such as weaker sections and low income groups at an affordable cost."

"Financial inclusion is a key path to poverty alleviation. In defining financial inclusion, it is important to see it as a progression and a hierarchy of financial needs which begins with the most basic needs, such as a secure account for holding payment transaction funds and bill payment, and moves to more complex ones such as *borrowing and insurance.*"

Financial inclusion, according to CAFRAL (2014) is the process of provision and ensuring timely access to a range of financial products and services at affordable costs by sound institutions in a fair and transparent manner to all sections of the society especially to the vulnerable groups such as weaker sections and low income groups.

Financial Inclusion in India

Further, financial inclusion, apart from opening and providing easy access to a No Frills account, should also provide access to credit, perhaps in the form of a General Credit Card (GCC) or limited OD against the no frills account. It should encompass access to affordable insurance and remittance facilities. It should also include credit counselling and financial education/ literacy.

Extent of Financial Inclusion: Financial Access Survey of IMF (2010), pointed out that the extent of financial exclusion is a global issue and relevant equally in the economies of the under-developed, developing and developed nations. The Financial Access Survey of IMF (2010) indicated the Indian Scenario on financial inclusion as given below. Enormity of the challenge of financial exclusion in India is that, almost half of the country is unbanked, even 4 decades after bank nationalization and extensive bank branch spread.

In India:

- 55% of the population has deposit accounts and 9% have credit accounts with banks.
- Highest number of households—145 million is excluded from Banking.
- There was one bank branch per 14,000 people.
- For about 6 lakh villages, rural branches of SCBs including RRBs numbered only 33,495.
- Less than 20% of the population has life insurance and 9.6% of the population has non-life insurance coverage.
- 18% had debit cards and less than 2 per cent had credit cards.

- 51.4% of farmer households are financially excluded from both formal and informal sources.
- Of the total farmer households, only 27% access formal sources of credit; one third of this group also borrowed from non-formal sources.
- Overall, 73% of farmer households have no access to formal sources of credit.

Across regions, financial exclusion is more acute in Central, Eastern and North-Eastern regions. All three regions together accounted for 64% of all financially excluded farmer households in the country. Overall indebtedness to formal sources of finance of these three regions accounted for only 19.66%. Several studies were conducted to assess the availability of credit in rural areas. They indicated that many of the rural households did not possess enough savings to meet even the basic expenses and accessibility to credit, hence become very crucial for the well—being of households. Kainth (2010) observed that the post nationalization period had enough pumping of credit to rural areas; there was a decrease in number of branches being opened in rural areas. It was found that delay in getting formal credit; non-availability of loan for domestic purposes and requirement of collateral by formal lending agencies are the major reasons that force households to take loans from informal markets.

An analysis of the extent of financial exclusion was made by CRISIL, indicated that across the states, financial exclusion is uneven and most of the states which fall under high exclusion category fall in the eastern, north-eastern and northern regions of the country. As per census 2011, only 58.7% of the households are availing banking services in the country.

Need for Financial Inclusion

Financial Inclusion may be defined as the process of ensuring access of financial services and timely, adequate credit where needed by vulnerable groups such as weaker sections and low income groups at an affordable cost.

Being included in the formal financial system helps people:

1. Make day-to-day transactions, including sending and receiving money.
2. Safeguard savings.

3. Finance small businesses or microenterprises, helping owners invest in assets and grow their businesses.
4. Plan and pay for recurring expenses, such as school fees.
5. Manage expenses related to unexpected events such as medical emergencies, a death in the family, theft, or natural disasters.
6. Improve their overall welfare.

The benefits of financial inclusion are not only significant for individuals but for economies as well. Financial inclusion is linked to a country's economic and social development, and plays a role in reducing extreme poverty.

Box 10.1: Having a Bank Account can Change a Woman's Life: Gates Report

The Bill & Melinda Gates Foundation praised India's efforts at digital financial inclusion, citing Aadhar as a system that has made banking simpler and more secure for the poor. The report called Goalkeepers. The Stories Behind the Data points out that two billion people worldwide still live completely outside the financial system. It references research conducted by Rohini Pande, professor public policy at Harward Kennedy School whose studies show that women who received wages in their own bank accounts worked more and saved more. Having used a bank account changed their sense of self, notes Pande, adding that they began describing their occupation as "worker" instead of "housewife".

The research also showed how payment banks in villages helped women access financial services easily, key factor in poverty elimination.

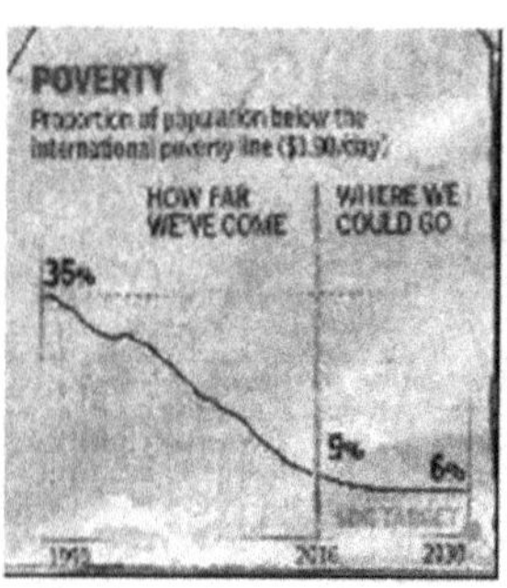

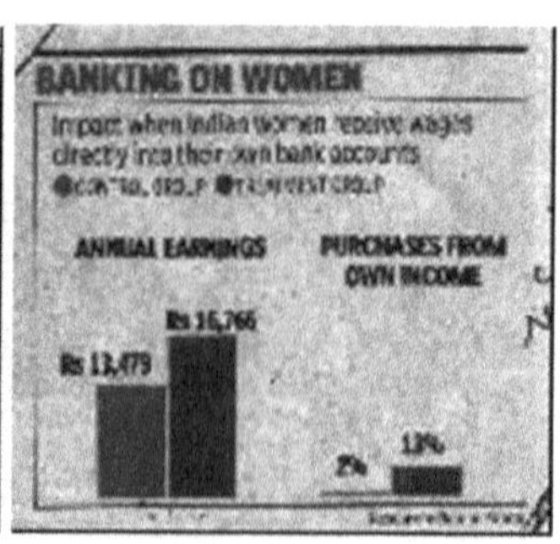

Impact when Indians receive wages directly into their own accounts.

Purchasesfromownincome increasedfrom 2%to 13%

Source: TOI, Sept.13, 2017.

Financial inclusion is of utmost importance for socio-economic development of poor and unbanked sections. It enables them to lessen their poverty levels through self-employment generation and promotes them as a part of banking system.

Approaches to Financial Inclusion—Some International/ National Initiatives

United Nations initiatives broadly described the main goals of inclusive finance as access to a range of financial services including savings, credit, insurance, remittance and other banking/payment services to all *'bankable'* households and enterprises at a reasonable cost.

The Report of the Centre for Global Development (CGD) Task Force on Access to Financial Services (October, 2009) 5 laid down the broad policy principles for expanding financial access, including institutional mechanisms, with particular emphasis on the need for ensuring data collection, monitoring and evaluation.

The G20 Toronto Summit (June, 2010) had outlined the "Principles for Innovative Financial Inclusion", and the parameters include: innovative, adequate, low-cost financial delivery models, a framework of incentives for the various bank, insurance, and non-bank actors involved in the delivery of a full range of affordable and quality financial services.

For example, in the United States, the Community Reinvestment Act (1977) requires banks to offer credit throughout their area of operation and prohibits them from targeting only the rich neighbourhood. The German Bankers' Association introduced a voluntary code in 1996 providing for an 'everyman' current banking account that facilitates basic banking transactions.

In South Africa, a low cost bank account called 'Mzansi' was launched for financially excluded people in 2004 by the South African Banking Association.

In the United Kingdom, a 'Financial Inclusion Task Force' was constituted by the government in 2005 in order to monitor the development of financial inclusion.

Different types of survey conducted to measure the financial access.

Table 10.1: Different Types of Survey Conducted to Measure the Financial Access

Type of survey	Definition	Survey objective	Examples
One time cross section	Cross section of pop is randomly selected and interviewed once	Snapshot of current level of financial access	❖ Finscope –All countries except for south Africa ❖ World Bank Access to Finance- 10 countries in total
Repeated cross section	Cross section of the population is randomly selected and interviewed once. In the next time period cross section of pop is interviewed	Monitor progress of financial access across time	❖ Finscope ❖ GFAS- Global demand side indicators to be collected every tow years ❖ Survey of consumer finances U.S.A multiyear approach used by U.S. Federal Reserve to assess consumer finance patterns.
Panel	The same households/ individuals are interviewed multiple times at regular intervals	Can be used to show a casual impact of changes in policy if combine with other factors.	❖ Financial Diaries- Household level survey conducted in 3 countries which studies the use of financial products and flow of financial services; conducted at the high frequency of every fortnight for one year ❖ ENNViH(family life survey)- Mexico: Conducted regularly; collects information on household income and expenditure; has some financial access questions, particularly credit.

History of Financial Inclusion in India:

1793 Formal distribution of Taccavi loans.

1883 Land Improvement Loans Act to finance agricultural loans to farmers to improve production

1904 Cooperative Credit Societies Act.

1928 Subsequent to the Royal Commission on Agriculture in India, Land Mortgage Banks were created.

1935 The Reserve Bank of India (RBI) set up its Agriculture Credit Department

1949 The RBI was nationalized

1955 The Imperial Bank was nationalized and renamed the State Bank of India

1963 The Agriculture Refinance Development Corporation was set up

1969 Nationalization of 14 Scheduled Commercial Banks

1970 Lead Bank Committee (F.K.F. Nariman) was formed

1972–76 Setting up of the Rural Electrification Corporation (REC), Small Farmer Development Agency (SFDA) and Regional Rural Banks (RRBs)

1981 Nationalization of 6 Scheduled Commercial Banks

1982 Creation of National Bank for Agriculture and Rural Development (NABARD)

1989 Service Area Approach (SAA) was initiated

1992 NABARD's Self Help Group (SHG)—Bank Linkage Policy

1996 Local Area Banks were set up

1997 Targeted Public Distribution System (TPDS) introduced

2005 Task Force on the Revival of Short Term Cooperative Credit Structure (STCCS)

2006 Policy initiative for Business Correspondents (BCs)/Business Facilitators (BFs)

2007 Committee on Financial Inclusion (C. Rangarajan)

2008 Agriculture Debt Waiver and Debt Relief Scheme

2009 The Mahatma Gandhi National Rural Employment Guarantee Act (MGNREGA) came into existence (NREGA since 2005)

2009 Formalization of the Unique Identification Number—Aadhaar

2013 Direct Benefit Transfer Scheme (DBT).

2014 Pradhan Mantri Jan Dhan Yojana (PMJDY).

The history of financial inclusion in India is actually much older than the formal adoption of the objective. The nationalization of banks, Lead Bank Scheme, incorporation of Regional Rural Banks, Service Area Approach and formation of Self-Help Groups—all these were initiatives aimed at taking banking services to the masses. The brick and mortar infrastructure expanded; the number of bank branches multiplied ten-fold—from 8,000+ in 1969, when the first set of banks were nationalized, to 99,000+ today. Despite this wide network of bank branches spread across the length and breadth of the country, banking has still not reached a large section of the population. The extent of financial exclusion is staggering. Out of the 600,000 habitations in the country, only about 36,000+ had a commercial bank branch. Just about 40 per cent of the population across the country has bank accounts. The proportion of people having any kind of life insurance cover is as low as 10 per cent and proportion having non-life insurance is abysmally low at 0.6 per cent. People having debit cards comprise only 13 per cent and those having credit cards only a marginal 2 per cent of the population.

The National Sample Survey data (2002–03) revealed that nearly 51 per cent of farmer households in the country did not seek credit from either institutional or non-institutional sources of any kind. A number of rural households are still not covered by banks. They are deprived of basic banking services like a savings account or minimal credit facilities. The proportion of rural residents who lack access to bank accounts is nearly 40 per cent, and the figure rises to over three-fifths in the eastern and north-eastern regions of India. Accordingly, our primary objective is to take banking to all excluded sections of the society, rural and urban.

A more focused and structured approach towards financial inclusion has been followed since the year 2005 when Reserve Bank of India decided to implement policies to promote financial inclusion and urged the banking system to focus on this goal. Our focus has, specifically, been on providing banking services to all the 600,000 villages and meeting their financial needs through basic financial products like savings, credit and remittance. The objectives of financial inclusion, in the wider context of the agenda for inclusive growth, have been pursued through a multi-agency approach. In 2006, the Government of India constituted a Committee on Financial Inclusion, which made a wide range of recommendations on the strategies for building an inclusive financial sector and gave a national rural financial inclusion plan. Government of India has set up the Financial Stability and Development Council (FSDC), which is mandated, inter alia, to focus on Financial Inclusion and Financial

Literacy Issues: In order to further strengthen the ongoing financial inclusion agenda in India, a high level Financial Inclusion Advisory Committee has been constituted by RBI. The Committee would pave the way for developing a viable and sustainable banking services delivery model focussing on accessible and affordable financial services, developing products and processes for rural and urban consumers presently outside the banking network and for suggesting appropriate regulatory framework to ensure that financial inclusion and financial stability move in tandem. Financial sector regulators including RBI are fully committed to the Financial Inclusion Mission.

Conclusion

The Current policy objective of Inclusive growth cannot be achieved without ensuring universal Financial Inclusion. Pursuit of financial inclusion by adoption of innovative products and processes poses challenge of managing trade-offs between the objective of financial inclusion and financial stability. The government has taken several initiatives to promote the pace of financial inclusion in the country but the need of the hour is to convert the threats into opportunities by utilizing the excessive population of the country in promoting financial inclusion, spreading financial literacy in the country and efforts be taken to bring the financially excluded in the scope of banking.

CHAPTER 11

Apex Institutions involved in Microfinance

Learning Objectives

1. To understand role of Apex Institutions in Facilitating MF lending
2. Policy Initiatives by Reserve Bank of India
3. Role of NABARD in promoting SHGs
4. Micro Credit Innovations Department
5. Role of Small Industries Development Bank of India
6. NGOs in facilitating MF
7. Bench Marking Microfinance and Microenterprises

Policy Initiatives by Reserve Bank of India (RBI)

RBI has taken a pro-active role in promoting microfinance. In 2002, it set up four Groups to look into various aspects of micro financing. Based on the recommendations of the various groups, RBI announced that banks would provide incentives to their branches, in making the procedures for financing the SHGs simple and easy. Based on the recommendations of the Vyas Committee, RBI indicated that microfinance institutions would not be permitted to accept public deposits (annual policy statement, 2004–05). An internal group of the RBI on Rural Credit and Microfinance under the Chairmanship of H.R. Khan, deputy governor, was set up to examine the issues relating to microfinance. A policy paper on "Development, Regulation and supervision of Micro-finance Services" was deliberated with the representatives of MFIs.

The SHG-Bank Linkage program is considered as a commercial proposition, with advantages of lower transaction costs, near zero NPA, an outreach to a wide rural population and business expansion in quantifiable terms.

National Bank for Agriculture and Rural Development (NABARD)

The National Bank for Agriculture and Rural Development (NABARD) was constituted in 1982 by an Act of Parliament. It's main objective was to provide credit for agriculture. Its vision is for fostering rural prosperity, through sustainable and equitable agriculture. It is the apex institution, for matters concerning policy, planning and operations in the field of credit for agriculture. It serves as an apex refinancing agency for the institutions providing investment and production credit in rural areas. In 1992, NABARD started a pilot project for commercial banks and cooperative banks to finance SHGs. Presently, the SHG-Bank Linkage Programme is the largest microfinance program in the world. It has a large outreach which encourages India's banks to lend to self-help groups (SHGs). The extent of participation can be realized by the fact that presently more than 100 scheduled banks, 349 DCCBs, 27 State Rural Livelihood Missions and over 5000 NGOs are engaged in promoting SHGs. Largely because SHGs are composed mainly of poor women, this has evolved into an important Indian tool for microfinance.

Till the 90s large sections of the rural population was unbanked and overlooked by the mainstream banking institutions. People in rural areas had to take recourse to informal sources of credit like the moneylender, who provided loans with least documentation. Further being in the same village the moneylender was accessible and available at any time. Another advantage was he offered flexible terms and loans for consumption needs like for marriage.

Inspite of the efforts of Government of India and RBI in creating and supporting enabling environment for increasing the outreach of formal financial services to cover the marginalized population, informal sector was popular.

In such a scenario, the Self Help Groups combined the flexibility and availability of informal sources with the transparency of institutional credit. The Self Help group—Bank Linkage Program (SHG-BLP) was an innovation by twinning the flexibility of the informal system with the strength and affordability of formal system. This saving led and door step credit delivery mechanism based on social collateral was supported by an enabling policy environment from national level institutions and multi-lateral agencies. The successful implementation of SHG-BLP established the credibility of groups as a bankable proposition SHG Bank Linkage program has traversed 25 years towards empowering the rural poor and rural women in particular. The pilot project has taken a big leap in becoming the largest community based microfinance covering more than a hundred million rural households

Women constitute almost half the population and make up one third of the labor force. Gender equality and women's empowerment is a fundamental goal of development, particularly microfinance groups. Muhammad Yunus' Grameen Bank gave an impetus to women's empowerment The Grameen Bank offered loans to women at a time when no one else would consider women as viable borrowers. NABARD started several projects geared directly towards women. Examples of these programs include: Gender Sensitization, Women Development Cell, Assistance to Rural Women in Rural Non-Farm Development (ARWIND), Assistance for Marketing of Non-Farm Products of Rural Women (MAHIMA), and Development of Women through Area Program (DEWTA). 26 In addition, women's groups constitute 90 percent of the SHG Linkage Program.

Micro Credit Innovations Department

Genesis

The Micro Credit Innovations Department under Nabard came into being in the year 1998 with the mainstreaming of the microfinance innovation i.e. SHG-Bank linkage programme on a nation-wide scale.

It is facilitating access to financial services for the unreached segments of the population viz. the poor in rural hinterlands. It is providing different products through various delivery channels in a cost effective and sustainable manner. Through the department, NABARD has continued its role as the facilitator and mentor of microfinance initiatives in the country.

Core Functions of the Department

NABARD has been continuously focusing on bringing in various stakeholders on a common platform and building their capacities to take the initiatives forward. This has resulted in tremendous growth of microfinance sector in India through different approaches like:

(a) Promotion of Self Help Group—Bank Linkage Programme (SHG-BLP) in the Country

Based on the observations of various research studies and an action research project carried out by NABARD, the model of 'SHG-BLP' was evolved as a cost effective mechanism for providing financial services to the unreached and underserved poor households. What started as a pilot to link around 500 SHGs of poor to the formal financial institutions during the year 1992–93, has now become the largest microfinance programme in the world, in terms of the client base and outreach.

The Cooperative and NGO sector has played a prominent role of working as a Self Help Group Promoting Institution (SHPI) by organizing, nurturing and enabling credit linkage of SHGs with banks. NABARD later co-opted many others as SHPIs including the rural financial institutions (RRBs, DCCBs, PACS, Farmers' Clubs (FCs), SHG Federations, NGO-MFIs, Individual Rural Volunteers (IRVs) etc.

These stakeholders were encouraged to take up promotion of SHGs by way of promotional grant assistance from NABARD. This savings-led microfinance model has now become the largest coordinated financial inclusion programme in the world covering almost 101 million households in the country. With more than 86% of the groups being exclusively women groups, the programme has provided a much needed push to women empowerment in the country.

(b) *Promotion of Joint Liability Groups (JLGs) and their financing by banks:*

JLGs are essentially credit groups of small/marginal/tenant farmers/asset less poor who do not have proper title of their farmland. These informal groups of 4–10 members are engaged in similar economic activities and are willing to jointly undertake to repay the loans taken by them from the Banks. Financing of JLGs was introduced as a pilot project in 2004–05 by NABARD in 8 States with the support of 13 RRBs. The scheme was later mainstreamed for the banking system in the year 2006.

Apart from extending refinance support of 100% to the financing Banks, NABARD also extends financial support for awareness creation and capacity building of all stakeholders under the Scheme. NABARD also extends start up grant support for formation and nurturing of JLGs to Banks and other JLG Promoting Institutions (JLGPIs).

Existing Role of the Department (NABARD)

NABARD continues to support and enable the entire ecosystem of support for the SHG-Bank linkage programme and other microfinance innovations. Following are some of the major functions under Self Help Group—Bank Linkage Programme (SHG-BLP):

- Innovating and making product level changes in the existing SHG product, improving risk mitigation systems, building second tier institutions of SHGs to address operational issues.
- Extending support to Cooperatives and NGOs for formation of SHGs and JLGs.
- Organizing and sponsoring large number of training and capacity building programmes, seminars and workshops for the benefit of all stakeholders viz. the bankers, the govt. agencies, and more importantly the SHG members themselves.
- *Livelihood promotion:* To enable the SHG members to take up livelihood activities, NABARD has been supporting Microenterprise Development Programmes (MEDPs) and Livelihood and Enterprise Development Programmes (LEDPs).
- WSHG scheme of GOI: NABARD is implementing and supporting the Women SHG scheme (WSHGs) announced by Govt. of India in backward and Left Wing extremism affected districts.
- *Digitisation of SHGs:* 'The department is making efforts to digitize the bookkeeping of SHGs by launching pilot project called E-Shakti across the country. The project has gone from strength to strength.
- Administration of Interest Subvention Scheme for Women SHGs under National Rural Livelihoods Mission (NRLM) of Ministry of Rural Development.

NABARD's Strategy for popularizing Microfinance: NABARD is adopting the following strategy to spread the outreach of SHG-Bank Linkage Programme.

1. Widening spatial distribution and intensity of the outreach of the Programme with district oriented planning and strategy.
2. Evolving district-wise plan of action/strategy in consultation with existing stakeholders aiming at promotion and linkage of a minimum of 500 SHGs per district every year.
3. Training and exposure programmes for the staff of the stakeholders.
4. Providing promotional assistance to partners for promoting and nurturing the SHGs generally an *add-on basis.*
5. Widening the range of SHG promoting agencies.
6. Involving banks at their corporate level, organizing training programmes for the regional/zonal managers of commercial banks in association with their Central Offices.
7. Establishing the financing of SHGs as a business proposition for banks.
8. Increasing the participation of the co-operative banks by encouraging them to financing SHGs as *financing cooperatives with the cooperatives.*
9. Associating village communities, people's institutions, rural volunteers and individuals to participate in the programme as SHG promoters.
10. Increasing the quality of the existing SHGs by propagating *self-rating* tools.
11. Large-scale dissemination of the concept and approach among the rural masses.
12. Encouraging the NGOs to play an important role in correcting the regional imbalances in spread of SHG-Bank Linkage Programme.

Small Industries Development Bank of India

SIDBI Foundation for Micro Credit (SFMC) was launched by the Bank in January 1999 for channelizing funds to the poor. Its mission was to create a national network of strong, viable and sustainable Microfinance Institutions (MFIs) for providing microfinance services to the economically disadvantaged people, especially women. Most microfinance programmes were initially operated by NGOs and were not subjected to regulation and supervision as they were registered as Societies or Trusts. Non-regulation of these institutions worked to their detriment and these institutions were not able to have smooth access to funds from the financial sector which was wary of lending to such entities. This constraint, posed a difficult challenge. Therefore, to meet the requirements of the revised dispensation which called for selection of suitable microfinance intermediaries which could be trusted with bulk assistance without collateral constraints, Capacity Assessment Rating [CAR] was introduced by SFMC as a supplementary tool to assess the risk perception. On SFMC's initiative, rating of MFIs was started by five agencies. With the passage of time, and ripening of the sector, most of the informal NGOs have transformed into formal NBFCs. Rating of MFIs has gained sector-wide acceptance and has become a pre requisite for getting assistance from the banks/financial institutions.

Financial Assistance

Microfinance: MFIs are provided annual need based assistance. One of the unique features of the scheme is the comprehensive financial support being provided to the MFIs/NGOs to expand their operations as well as to increase their efficiency. SIDBI's support comprises of loans as well as equity/quasi equity support, as the case may be, depending on the need of the client institutions.

Missing Middle Segment: SIDBI has also been extending financial assistance for the Missing Middle Segment of the microenterprises. In India, 'Missing Middle' connotes the financing gap that lies above micro-finance loans and below traditional institutional financing i.e., loans with financial volumes ranging from INR 50,000 to INR 10 lakh. The support under this scheme is channelized through Participating Financial Institutions (NBFCs, RRBs, UCBs, MFIs, etc.).

Minimal Security Requirement

Credit worthiness is based on the rating of the borrowing institutions rather than availability of security/collateral requirements. Term Deposit Receipts (TDRs) issued by Scheduled Commercial Banks/SIDBI for an amount equivalent to 10%/5% are taken (depending upon geographical area of operation, categories of beneficiaries supported and duration of partnership of the MFI with SIDBI etc.)

Portfolio Risk Fund (PRF)

Portfolio Risk Fund (PRF) was created by SIDBI with funding support from Government of India and made operational since March 2004. Normally, the Bank stipulates security requirement of FDRs. equivalent of up to 10% of the loan sanctioned to MFIs under SFMC dispensation. Once the case is covered under PRF, 75% of security requirement (i.e. 7.5% of the loan amount) is booked under PRF and balance 25% (i.e. 2.5% of the loan amount) only is to be furnished by the individual MFI by way of FDRs.

India Microfinance Equity Fund (IMEF)

To ease the tight liquidity situation, in the FY 2012, GoI stepped in with creation of a Rs. 100 crore Fund viz., IMEF, operated through SIDBI, to strengthen capitalization of smaller, socially oriented MFIs, especially in underserved states/areas. The allocation under IMEF has been increased by Rs. 200 crore in FY 2013–14. The assistance under the Fund is expected to help the MFIs leverage more debt funds from the banks and financial institutions and help in increased flow of assistance to the poor in the unserved/underserved areas of the country.

Sa-Dhan

Sa-Dhan's mission is to build the field of community development finance in India to help its member and associate institutions to better serve low-income households, particularly women, in both rural and urban India, in their quest for establishing stable livelihoods and improving quality of life. Founded as the Association of Community Development Finance Institutions by SEWA Bank, BASIX, Dhan Foundation, FWWB, MYRADA, RGVN, SHARE and PRADAN in 1999. Sa-Dhan's membership has now grown to 251 with the collective loan outstanding and outreach in excess of Rs. 18,343 Crores and 26.7 million poor, respectively. The Microfinance sector in India is still evolving and witnessing increasing entry of new players. Hence, Sa-Dhan as the designate national association of Community Development Finance Institutions (CDFIs) represents an "emerging but rapidly growing sector". Given the nascent nature of the sector, Sa-Dhan has a crucial role to play in increasing capacities, affecting the evolution and adoption of best practices, increasing the number of service providers and contributing to improving the policy and operational context for Microfinance in India. Its objectives are to:

- To provide a common platform for advocacy representing multiple models and approaches to microfinance in India.
- To make available timely and reliable information that is crucial for effective networking of microfinance institutions across India.
- To undertake research, development of tools and resources that facilitate dialogue and synergy of best practices between different operating models and stakeholders.
- To promote initiatives that inform, educate and articulate the needs of the sector. These programs will involve service providers, policy makers and bankers.
- To provide technical and marketing support systems for sustainable livelihoods through community development finance.

NGOs in Facilitating MF

Friends of Women's World Banking

FWWB was promoted in 1981, as an affiliate of Women's World Banking, a global network created to focus on the need for women's direct access to financial services and recognizing women's role in building a nation's economy.

FWWB combined its loans with technical assistance to ensure sustainable growth and from 1989 to 2010 it has reached out to more than 300 Microfinance Institutions (MFIs) with technical assistance and nearly 200 with loan support. FWWB has successfully implemented programs with support from SIDBI, FORD Foundation, Citi Foundation, HIVOS, CORDAID, USAID, Micheal and Susan Dell Foundation and many more and access loan support from 10 plus banks and financial institutions.

Initially started as a capacity building institution, FWWB had decided to provide loan support to different type of institutions (SHGs, Federations, Cooperatives, NGOs and startup NBFCs) that are in the space of financial inclusion. Luke warm response from the banking sector to support these institutions was the reason for building the revolving loan fund and taking the risk as a first lender. Support from bilateral, international as well as local institutions enabled FWWB to scale up and support more than 300 institutions across the country in areas of livelihood promotion, water and sanitation, education and women empowerment. FWWB was instrumental in organizing various policy forums focusing on financial services for the poor and played a very active role in policy advocacy. FWWB, being a member of various networks, has played a significant role in the building of the sector. Cumulatively FWWB has reached out to more than 1 million women across India through its various interventions.

Benchmarking Microfinance and Microenterprises

What is Benchmarking?

Benchmarking is establishing standards of excellence in working of any organizations. This is the highest standard for efficiency and effectiveness in work organization. Benchmarking in Microfinance and Microenterprise practices refers to those organizations who have excellent work practices, culture and are able to outperform other similar organizations. The next few chapters illustrates such organizations.

Section-II

Case Studies

CHAPTER 12

Antodaya—Unto the Last

Introduction

The father of the nation Mahatma Gandhi, spearheaded the Antodaya movement in serving the poor and downtrodden. Today, the same idea is carried forward by cooperative institutions by dispensing credit to the "poorest of the poor". The Core Group on SHG's' (Self Help Groups) from Maharashtra had an exposure visit to Bidar District Cooperative Central Bank to study the PACs SHG model. The case Profile of Bidar District Co-operative Bank illustrates how the Primary Agricultural Societies through SHGs have helped in uplifting the socio-economic standards of the disadvantaged people.

Bidar district is the northern most district of the Karnataka State, with a population of 1.4 million in 600 villages. It is a remote & backward district in Karnataka. Only 10% of land is irrigated. 52% of the 2,80,000 families are below poverty and 30% belong to SC/ST. A major part of the district is in the Godavari river basin and a small portion is in the Krishna basin. The district has 5 talukas, Aurad, Bidar, Bhakli, B. Kalyan and Humnabad.

The Bidar DCCB has completed 50 years since its establishment in 1952. It has been successful in meeting the credit needs of the farmers through the medium of its 171 member Primary Agriculture Cooperative Societies (PACs). The bank has through it's network of 41 branches dispensing credit services to rural families. The progress of the bank is given in Annexure 1 & 2. The bank has been consistently earning profits since last 10 years, and got best performance award in 1998–99, 1999–2000 and 2000–2001.

The bank found that despite a wide network, a large section of society comprising of landless labourers, poor artisans and others living below the poverty line were still not covered by any financial institutions. "Keeping this in mind, the board of directors of the bank in the annual meeting of the diamond jubilee decided to assist the poor who do not have any collateral to give as security for the loans and therefore depend on moneylenders" explained Shri Gurupadappa Nagamarpalli, President of Bank. In order to reach the rural poor, the bank decided to extend the assistance through the self-help groups. To start with in 1997 the bank provided loans to the SHGs promoted by the two main NGOs of the district; PRAWARDA and 'Mahila Samakhya'. When all these groups repaid the loan fully without any follow up, the bank decided to promote SHGs and link them through the Primary Agriculture Cooperative Societies (PACs).

After observing the success of the loans provided by the bank to the SHGs promoted by the two NGOs, the bank decided to undertake SHG promotion activity as a part of its business portfolios. The primary objectives of initiating the SHG linkage as a normal activity of the bank were:

- To provide assistance to the rural poor who had been deprived of the facility of the formal banking system through the network of PACs.
- To take up SHG promotion as a strategy for the revitalization of the PACs.
- To fulfil the social objective of serving the poor.
- To develop non-farm sector through the medium of SHGs.

Initial Experiments in Microfinance

By 1997, Bidar, DCC bank, had covered more than 80% of the farmers under the credit facility. However, another major segment of rural families (about 1.40 lakh families) were unreached by the formal credit systems.

The Board of Directors of the DCCB had an exposure visit to MYRADA at Kamalapur in Gulbarga district to study the concept and functioning of SHGs. MYRADA is one of the pioneers in the SHG movement in India. After seeing the functioning and development of the SHGs at Kamalapur, the management were convinced about the opportunity to reach the unreached rural poor families that can be provided with not only credit support but also support for changing their social, economical and educational status through the concept of SHG.

An SHG cell was opened with 3 officers who had worked in NGOs for formation of SHGs. These officers did intensive field work in Bhosga area and formed 23 SHGs. These SHGs were handed over to the PACs, after training the PACs secretaries and the Branch Managers.

DCCB Bidar considered this experiment as a Pilot Project and the lessons learnt during the initial period gave some more insight regarding the strategy to be adopted. The bank decided to strengthen 171 PACs as Self Help Promoting Institutions (SHPIs) which would eventually form, train, develop and link the SHGs to their PACs. Humnabad Taluk was the first Taluk wherein every village and hamlet had at least one SHG and was declared as a SHG Taluka by the Governor of Karnataka.

Table 12.1: SHG Progress Report as on 31/12/02 Bidar DCCB

1.	Total number of SHGS formed in the district	6352
	(a) SHGs formed by PACs	2052
	(b) NGOs	2566
	(c) Shree Shakti	1734
2.	Total SHG members	1,00,945
3.	No. of women members	96,998
4.	Cumulative Internal savings mobilized (in lakhs)	1,196,005
5.	No. of SHGs financed by DCCB	3911
6.	Amount of Loan given by DCCB (in lakhs)	1036.685
7.	% Recovery	98%

Interest rate on SHG loans.

Source: Micro Credit Division, Bidar DCCB.

The success is due to the coordinated efforts of DCCB Bidar and NGOs in the District. Encouraged by the progress made in the field of Microfinance, the DCCB prepared an action plan to have more than 3 SHGs in every village/hamlets and more than 20 SHGs in every PACs area by March 2002–03. By now all the villages and hamlets have at least one SHG and Bidar district will shortly be declared as "SHG district".

SHG Banking: By December 2002, a total of 6352 SHGs had been established in Bidar District. Comprising about 100,000 member from poor families. 5005 SHGs had opened savings accounts with DCCB, and 3911 had been credit linked.

Table 12.2: SHGs Linked to DCCB by Self Help Promoting Agency (SHPI) 31/3/2002

SHP I	*SHGs with Savings Accounts*		*SHGs with Loan Accounts*	
	Number	*%*	*Number*	*%*
PACS	1866	37	1123	36
NGOs	2374	47	1345	43
Womens org. (Stree Shakti)	76.5	15	649	21
Total	**5005**	**99%**	**3117**	**100**

Institutionalizing SHG Banking

The bank has established a separate Micro Credit Division. It's head, Mr. Siddhaling Kumar, said "The division has trained all branch and PACs staff. It has developed PACs as SHPIs and as an instrument of sustainable SHG promotion at the grassroots level."

Of the bank's 43 branches, 40 participate in SHG Banking. The branch of Bhosga, acts as an intermediary for 6 PACs, where 129 SHGs hold their accounts.

The PACs provide financial services to 69 SHGs. 43 of them have loans outstanding. SHG deposits account for 380/0 of outstanding, which is identical to the share of overall deposits in overall outstanding. Non-performing loan in the PACs are coming down, but are still high at 3.60/0. In contrast, NPLs are zero in the cooperative's lending to SHGs. The PACs earns 1.50/0 on its total assets and 2.00/0 on its SHG assets. The PACs attribute much of the change over the last three years to its participation in SHG linkage banking and its indirect effects on cooperative members: an increase in deposits from Rs. 1.3 m to Rs. 3.5 m an increase in loans outstanding from Rs. 4.1m to Rs. 9.1 m and increase in the recovery from 910/0 to 940/0. There is a new, awakening that the society accepts deposits: 12 out of 113 fixed deposit holders are SHG members. The figures for the PACs at Ladwanthi are shown below in Table 3, and they are indicative of the trend.

Table 12.3

PACS, Ladwanthi (31/3/2012)	*SHG*	*PACS*
Total assets (in Rs. 1000)	1,320	12,503
Net loans outstanding (in Rs. 1000)	1,262	9,131
Deposits	481	3,254
Non-performing loans	0%	3.6%
Return on average assets (ROA)	2.0%	1.5%
Operational self-sufficiency (CGAP)	116%	113%

Profitability of SHG Banking

SHG Banking is breaking even (with a slight positive margin) at bank level, where the overhead costs for the Microcredit Division are borne, while the bulk of the profit-making SHG business is shifted to the branches and PACs. The relevant figures for the Bidar DCCB, its Bhosga branch and the PACs Ladwanthi are given below in Table 4.

Table 12.4: Profitability of SHG Banking, 31/3/2002

Unit	*ROA*
DCCB	0.1%
Branch of Bhosga	4.2%
PACs of Ladwanthi	2.5%

Impact on SHG Savings, Retained Earnings and Borrowings

There is a strong impact of SHG membership on saving behavior. In many SHGs, the amount of individual weekly savings has quadrupled from Rs. 5 to Rs. 20, which has substantially increased the volume of loanable funds and retained earnings. As of August 2002, SHGs in the district had total savings of Rs. 120 m and retained earnings of Rs. 90 m (common fund), totaling internal resources of Rs. 210 m, which is nearly five times the amount of bank loans of Rs. 45 m. The total working capital is thus Rs. 255 m (US $5.26 m). The annual total turnover of SHGs is reportedly Rs. 500 m. The repayment rate is 98%; non-performing loans are zero.

Table 12.5

Resources of SHGs in Bidar District, Auz. 2002	*Amounts*	
	Million Rs.	*Million $*
Savings	120	2.50
Retained Earnings	90	1.88
Total internal resources	210	4.33
Bank loans	45	0.93
Total resources	255	5.26

The proportion of SHG deposits in terms of loans outstanding in the three entities studied is as follows:

Bidar DCCB consolidated : 27%
Branch of Bhosga : 93%
PACs of Ladwanthi : 38%

Benefits of SHG Banking

1. Indirect benefits of SHG Banking in the district are pronounced. 38% of the families in the district, and 72% of poor families are SHG members with access to financial resources.
2. Empowerment of women, who are increasingly involved in community development programs and local politics.
3. Exposure of bad habits of family members harassment of women, resulting changing male attitudes and behavior.
4. Exposure of social evils such as child marriage, child labour and dowry.

Impact at PACs Level

Training is an integral part of the whole process and the Board of Directors, Secretaries, Accountants and other staffs of PACs have been trained on SHG concept and it's functioning. This motivated the PACs to promote, develop and finance SHGs. At present there are 1993 SHGs promoted by the PACs themselves of them 929 SHGs are financed by DCCB as on November, 2001.

The Micro Credit Division (MCD) of the Bank has established good rapport with Zilla Panchayat and Government Departments at district and Taluk level as a result, the Block Development Officers and other government officials have been supporting the programme.

The DCC Bank intends to make PACs to play the role of NGOs in the promotion and financing of SHGs and PACs have also realized the advantages in SHG promotion and linkage. They are benefited as the DCCB is paying interest margin to PACs on SHG loans @ 1.5% p.a. that will also improve the financial position of PACs by increase in saving bank deposits, increase in lending, and higher recovery percentage.

The monthly monitoring of SHGs is done by the MCD. Table 12.6 shows the monthly progress report on promotion and credit linkage of self help groups as on 31/12/02.

Table 12.6: Performance Figures of SHGs

(A)	*Promotion Figures of SHGs*		
Sl. No.	*Particulars*		*No. of SHGs*
1.	SHGs promoted up to the end of the previous year. of (a) No. of Women SHGs		5005 4792
2.	SHGs Promoted during the Current Year (i.e. from 1 April to the end of the reporting month) a. By PACs b. By NGOs c. By Stree Shakti d. Total		 186 192 969 1347
3	e. of (d) of women SHGs Cumulative No. of SHGs promoted (L.el)(a)+2(d)		1347 6352
4.	Of 3 above, No. of SHGs more than 6 months old		5920
5.	Total no. of women SHGs (L.e l(b)+ 2(e)		6139
(B)	*Cumulative internal savings mobilised by SHGs (As at the end of reporting Month)*		*1196.005*
(C)	*Credit Linkage of SHGs Number*		*Amount of loan*
	Credit Linkage during the current year		*Disbursed*

	SHGs promoted By:		*(Rs. Lakhs)*
1.	a. PACs b. NGOs c. Stree Shakti d. Total e. Of (d) women SHGs	304 155 335 794 794	104.855 124.45 50.66 279.965 279.965
2.	Cumulative Credit Linkage (Since inception till the end of reporting month) SHGs promoted by a. PACs b. NGOs c. Stree Shakti d. Total	 1427 1353 1131 3911	 361.475 526.47 148.77 1036.715
	e. Of (d) women SHGs	3830	979.205

Revitalisation of PACS by SHG Promotion

With the introduction of SHG concept at the PACs level through proper training to the non-officials and staff of PACs, they can be converted, as SHPIs and will have the following impact on the functioning of the PACs.

1. As more and more SHG SB A/c are opened in the PACs, the day-to-day operations in the PACs increases.
2. The SHG members will come to the PACs for depositing their savings.
3. This will create an environment of day-to-day banking in the PACs by which the operational efficiency of the PACs improves.
4. The SB Deposit in PACs will increase. For example in Bhemalkhed PACs, 70 SHGs are saved an amount of 3.4 lakhs and out of which 1.03 lakhs is balance in the SB account.
5. This amount is used by many PACs for business due to which they have saved the interest payable on cash credit limit earlier being availed from DCCB.
6. This will also ensure regular presence of the secretary of the PACs that leads to social auditing by the people in the villages.
7. The lending and profit of PACs has increased. For example in Bhemalkhed PACs, 24 SHGs were given loan of Rs. 8.36 lakhs

during the period 1996–2000. The PACs has earned more than Rs. 12,500/- of interest margin.
8. The risk involved is nil, as there is 100% repayment of loan. The operational cost is negligible.
9. Promotion of SHGs improves the repayment ethics of not only the. SHG members (most of whom are women) but also the other borrowers.
10. There are instances of repayment of overdue by the non-SHG borrowers as they see the poor families repaying the loans.
11. The lending in the PACs has increased substantially where as operational cost has reduced to a greater extent.
12. The SHG movement has helped to strengthen the Business Development Plan (BDP) of PACs.

About the Author

Professor, Vaikunth Mehta National Institute of Cooperative Management, Pune–411 007.

A "Core Group on SHGs" was constituted by Shri Ratnakar Gaikwad Commissioner & RCS, Cooperative Societies, Maharashtra in September 2002. The author was a member of the Core Group.

Published in "The Administrator", Vol. 46, No. 1, July, 2013.

Annexure I: Performance Figures of Bidar DCCB (Figures in Rs. Lakhs)

Year	*No. of Members*	*Paid up and Other Reserves*	*Statutory*	*Borrowings*	*Deposit*	*Loans & Advance O/s*	*Working Capita*	*Investment*	*Net Profit*
1975	410	139.36	32.09	464.18	158.41	745.86	828.28	66.56	8.94
1980	334	168.88	85.39	327.46	359.52	786.81	1005.52	163.99	15.85
1985	339	193.78	154.84	625.22	681.69	1386.49	1823.47	192.48	24.93
1990	338	232.71	251.27	780.04	1613.12	1965.35	3073.22	415.85	1.22
1991	344	246.54	257.75	1341.30	1669.65	2888.31	3794.37	406.65	14.83
1992	350	256.19	282.96	1268.81	2061.44	2774.52	4271.63	516.59	28.19
1993	350	286.38	307.60	1262.79	2491.26	3177.50	4621.70	625.69	31.36
1994	352	260.73	328.87	1731.61	2978.84	4288.56	5735.95	830.17	36.30
1995	358	383.26	343.33	2595.56	3329.11	5102.71	7195.35	914.23	42.46
1996	366	495.51	523.60	3687.71	4106.68	6751.85	9263.43	1371.16	5171
1997	377	552.77	659.17	5301.05	5215.74	9215.02	12174.28	1844.01	62.55
1998	380	642.88	837.59	5813.91	7474.09	11603.82	15393.04	2299.81	111.16
1999	380	789.31	1056.16	6150.43	12190.73	15604.59	20972.20	3394.81	189.49
2000	380	899.87	1339.64	7574.45	16529.92	20590.96	27367.76	4366.81	224.50
2001	384	994.01	1629.94	10987.31	21183.13	27121.06	35960.71	5895.52	303.02
2002	384	1119.92	1954.51	14966.45	24904.06	34243.34	44383.96	5653.52	328.30

Annexure II: Some Performance Figures of Bidar DCCB

Sr. No.	*Particulars*	*1996–97*	*1997–98*	*1998–99*	*1999–00*	*2000–01*	*2001–02*
1.	Recovery	75%	69%	80%	81%	84%	89%
2.	Profit (Amount)	62.55	111.15	189.49	226.96	303.02	328.00
3.	Average Field on Assets (%)	13.37	13.49	12.93	13.13	13.12	12.98
4.	Average cost of Funds (%)	8.77	8.60	8.47	8.80	9.42	9.64
5.	Financial Margin (%)	4.60	4.89	4.46	4.27	3.70	3.34
6.	Cost of (%) Management	3.00	3.11	2.61	2.46	2.39	1.38
7.	Net Margin (%)	1.35	1.35	1.64	1.38	1.40	1.55
8.	No. of Branch Productivity	41	42	43	41	41	41
9.	Per Branch Productivity	280.93	454.20	507.63	863.13	1123.33	1375.52
10.	Per Employee Productivity	50.30	94.92	113.10	191.31	255.58	326.78

CHAPTER 13

Professor Yunus and the Grameen Model

ABSTRACT

This article traces the beginning of the business model adopted by the Grameen Bank under the leadership of Prof Md. Yunus. It also discusses the findings/observations of the authors in course of an exposure visit to Bangladesh. All those involved in the microfinance sector can surely draw a number of lessons from her experience.

Prof. Yunus has become an iconic figure in micro credit, after the Nobel Peace prize was conferred on him and the Grameen Bank in 2006. It was to see this wonderful work of his that I led an exposure visit of trainees to sensitize them to the philosophy and operations of Grameen Bank. The group comprised of the Chairmen and Directors of Apex and District Cooperative banks, urban banks and cooperative societies from Maharashtra, Gujarat, Kamataka, Orissa and West Bengal.

In 1992, the National Agriculture and Rural development Board (NABARD), had initiated a pilot project on Self Help Groups and Bank Linkage Program. Since then Commercial Banks, and Cooperative banks have been forming Self Help Groups (SHGs). According to NABARD estimates, there are 2 million SHGs financed by banks covering 164.9 million poor families. The credit disbursed is Rs. 1.8 million. It has been promoted as a "viable banking proposition", and a win-win situation where the bank's recovery position is also improved. This novel idea of lending to a group was conceived by Prof Yunus.

On Day one we had a briefing session addressed by Shri Dipal Barua, the Deputy Managing Director of Grameen Bank. He traced the early days when he was a student of economics of Prof. Yunus at the Chittagong University. As Prof. Yunus has expressed in his writings that he found it hard to teach classroom theories in economics when there was so much poverty all around him! In 1974 there was a terrible famine in Bangladesh, and he wanted to do something to help the poor people around him. It is this intrinsic quality of Prof. Yunus to help the poor that started him on this mission. Perhaps this is the quality of *generosity of heart and empathy* that one has to have before one can think of doing this kind of work.

Prof. Yunus was shocked to discover a woman borrowing US$O.25 with the condition that the lender will have the exclusive right to buy all she produces at the price the lender decides! He made a list of the victims of money lending "business" in the Jobra village and found that 42 victims had borrowed US $ 27. It was a spontaneous thought that occurred to him of offering the money from his own pocket to get the victims out of the clutches of the moneylender. This act of humanity propelled him to help more of the poor. He approached the banker on the campus to lend to the poor, but the bankers said that "The poor are not credit worthy"! Prof. Yunus then offered to stand as guarantor for the loans of the poor. He was stunned to find that the poor paid back their loans, contradicting the views held by the Bankers ! In fact the "poor *are* credit worthy"!

Banking without Collateral

One of the Chairmen in our group said "our society has lot of surplus, but women are not ready to borrow when we ask them for collateral!" Conventional banks insist on security from borrowers; but poor and asset less people have no security to give, and thus remain "un-reached" by banks It was because of this rigid attitude of the bankers that, Prof. Yunus thought of creating a bank for the poor. In 1983, he set a separate bank for the poor to give loans without collateral. This was how the Grameen Bank came into existence.

Today the Grameen Bank has a formidable presence all over Bangladesh and countries around the world. It is reaching 7.7 million poor borrowers, 96% of whom are women. Grameen bank has 2,475 branches working in 90 per cent of the villages in Bangladesh. The amount of funds disbursed is US$ 8 billion. The loan recovery rate is 99.01%.

Institutional Set Up

When he had come to India, Prof. Yunus observed that there is no institutional set up in the micro sector.

Bipal Barua explained the institutional set up of Grameen Bank. Every village has a grameen or village centre where women gather for their meetings. Each Centre has 10 to 12 groups; and every Group has 5 to 10 women members of the same village. The Centre in-Charge talks to the women and collects their savings to open an account in the Grameen Branch. Every Branch has 10–12 village centres under their jurisdiction. The Branch Manager holds two meetings in every village every morning. He then goes to the branch in the afternoon where he disburses the money to the borrowers. Every branch has an Area Office, with 10 to 12 branches under their supervision. Such an arrangement ensures flexibility and contact up to the grass root borrowers in the village. Area Offices are in turn reporting to Zonal Offices; and the Zonal Offices report to the Head office.

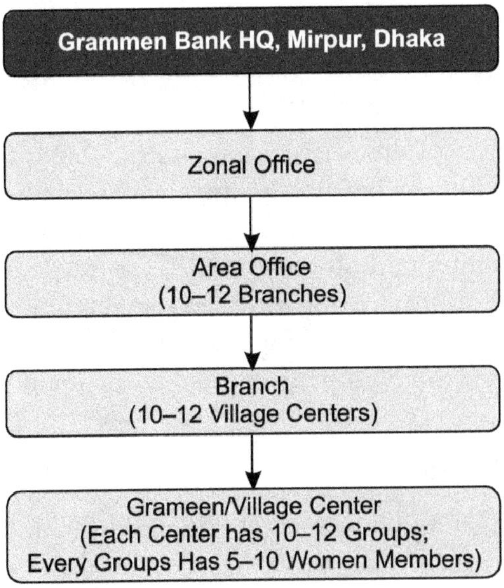

Fig. 13.1

The Grameen Bank arranged field trips for us so that we could be properly exposed to the philosophy and procedures of Grameen Bank.

We visited the Grameen Centre at Sadipur Sonargaon, about 35 kms from Dhaka. However crossing the city with its notorious traffic jam, took us an hour and a half. The roads are crowded with rickshaw pullers, buses and big sized cars like Toyota Corolla, Pajero, Tata and the like. On either side, the roads were lined by furniture, lubrication and repair, and sweetmeat shops. But after taking the turn to the interior, the vast green fields swaying with paddy and mustard fields were very soothing to the eye.

On the way we were joined by the Grameen Branch Manager. The car took a turn on a small brick lined bund and came to halt at a cluster of tin roofed houses. We were taken to the Grameen Centre, where women had gathered enthusiastically to greet us. Anwar, the officer introduced us in Bengali as guests who have come from India, to see and interact with you. The Grameen group leader introduced herself and narrated how almost 22 years back she came to know of Grameen Bank from friends. She had taken an initial loan of 3000 taka for basket weaving. Now her grown up sons are having a medicine shop in the market, another is having a laundry and the third is running a transport company. It is therefore rightly believed that when money is given to the woman, the benefits will be spread to other family members; unlike men who are likely to spend on their personal cravings. From all these activities her monthly installment now is 10,000 takas.

We then strolled to the neighboring houses. One lady was dexterously weaving a cane basket. The surroundings were kept neat and clean. So also the houses inside were neatly and tidily maintained. The walls were lined with mud, but the roofs were of tin. On enquiring why, we were told that it is safe from rain and tin sheets are commonly used as house construction material. The cooking stove was outside the house and a little further was the toilet properly covered to maintain privacy.

The "Sixteen Decisions"

Early in the program, borrowers of Grameen Bank were engaged in intensive dialogues at the village level to reflect on their lives. Some of these dialogues generated decisions that covered many subjects, but gave high priority to health (drinking water, nutrition, housing, hygiene, family planning, cleanliness), social;(sending their children to school, keeping the center free from dowry, not practice child marriage, and collectively fight any injustice as also take part in all social activities collectively) and economic; for higher incomes collectively undertake bigger investments. These "Sixteen Decisions" have become an integral part of Grameen Bank. Many borrowers recite the decisions and all are required to make continuous efforts to implement these decisions. This we could see from their awareness of keeping their houses and surroundings clean By the side of the embankment, the scene was idyllic; the ducks swam in the river and across the river we saw fields growing vegetables like cauliflower, potatoes, carrots and men harvesting the gourd, loading it in their small boats to take it to the city market.

Local Bodies Representation

Grameen system makes the borrowers familiar with the election process. They routinely go through electing group chairperson and secretaries, centre-chiefs and deputy centre-chiefs every year. They elect Board members of the Grameen Bank every three years. This experience has prepared them to run for public offices, as they are now confident to contest and get elected in the local governments.

Disbursement of Loans

We then went to the Sadirpur Sonargaon Branch. The red brick building was one of the oldest having 5 stars, the significance of which was later explained by the Manager. Seated in the main hall the Manager showed us one of the loan proposals. Most of it was in Bengali so we could not read it. But the Manager collects loan proposals from the Grameen Centre. After examining the amount of loan, it's purpose borrowers capability to repay, the Manager gives the loan amount. In the afternoon 'Nomen come to receive the disbursements. The loans are promptly disbursed by the Branch Manager in a week's time! The loans are borrower-centric. It is the borrower's ability to generate income and repayment capacity is the sole criteria in the disbursal of loans. Grameen Bank finances 100 per cent of its outstanding loan from its deposits. Over 64 per cent of its deposits come from bank's own borrowers.

Housing for the Poor

The Housing loans introduced in 1984, became a very attractive program for the borrowers. This program was awarded Aga Khan International Award for Architecture in 1989. Maximum amount given for housing loan is US $ 219. Interest rate is 8 per cent. Here is a very interesting anecdote which Prof. Yunus shared with us on why these loans have become popular. In the Islamic religion, it is easy for men to divorce their wives by repeating "talaq" thrice. However, when women started having houses in their names, the men were forced to think twice before saying "talaq"; as they would otherwise be compelled to leave the house!

Microenterprise Loans

Grameen Bank provides larger loans called micro-enterprise loans for fast moving members. Power tiller, irrigation pumps, transport vehicle, river craft for transportation and fishing are popular items on which livelihoods are based and are supported by micro-enterprise loans. They help to increase the earning capacity of the member.

There is no restriction on the loan size, but the repayment installments are pre-decided by the borrower.

Life Insurance and Pension Fund

Borrowers come under this insurance coverage by being a shareholder of the bank. Families of deceased borrowers of Grameen Bank receive life 'insurance benefits. Moreover, borrowers are not required to pay any premium for this life insurance. As borrwers grow older, they worry about what will happen to them when they cannot work and earn anymore. Grameen Bank addressed this issue by introducing the Pension fund for old age. Under this program, the borrower saves a small amount, about (Tk 500, over a period of 10 years; after which she gets almost twice the amount of money she has saved. The borrowers find this very attractive!

Management Information System

The Grameen Communications has developed a simple software to maintain the accounts of the Branch at the Area Office. Accounting and information management of 2,395 branches has been computerized. This has freed the branch staff to devote more time to the borrowers, rather than spend it on paper work. Branch staff are provided with printed repayment figures for each weekly meetings. If the borrower pays according to the repayment schedule, the staff has nothing to write on the document, except putting his signature. Only the deviations are recorded. Paper work that remains to be done at the village level, is to enter figures in the borrower's pass book.

Grameen Shakti

To encourage renewable energy the Grameen Shakti was launched in 1994. We visited a solar unit in Shingair. Mr Islam was the young engineer in charge of the unit. He explained how there are three packages which provide electricity for four hours to run the light, and fan.

Women spend long hours in front of the stove, To give them a clean environment, the improved gas stove was developed which ensures that the smoke and dust are let off through a chimney. We were also shown the biogas unit.

Grameen Technology Centre

We met three young girls who had done an engineering course from the technical institutes and were working at the Centre as Instructors. Every course was of 15 days. They train the borrowers to repair mobile chargers, inverters, and other electronic components.

Telephone Ladies

Grameen Bank has provided loans to 2,94,801 women borrowers to buy mobile phones and offer telecommunication services in nearly half of the villages of Bangladesh; where this service never existed before. These telephone-ladies run a very profitable business with these phones, and at the same time play an important role in the telecommunication sector of the country, and also generating revenue for Grameenphone. As the country is disaster prone due to typhoons and floods, even if the landlines go dead, these ladies remain active in the villages!

Grameen Shikha

The next day we visited the Shingair branch. Among the women gathered were some members who had taken loans for education of their children.

While most of the older women borrowers were 5th or 7th pass, they had taken education loans for their children to pursue higher education. This is a wonderful scheme to give opportunities for higher studies. The education loans bear no interest till a year after the beneficiary completes his/her education; after which the interest charged is 8.5%. Some remarkable case studies were told how in the face of social handicaps one girl Nasir studied for medicine, and is now aspiring to be a gynecologist. It is a new hope for the children of mothers who were illiterate! Prof. Yunus does not want the younger generation to take up wage employment. On the other hand he urges them to become professionals or set up microenterprises, which in turn would generate employment for others!

Struggling (Beggars) Members Programme

Is it "idealism" which makes Prof Yunus dream of eradicating poverty in Bangladesh by 2013; or as he says "putting poverty into museums"? Or to make sure that no one in the Grameen Bank villages has to beg for survival.

To reach out to the beggars, Grameen Bank has taken up a special program called "Struggling Members Programme" from July 2002. The objective of the program is to provide financial services to the beggars to help them find a dignified livelihood, send their children to school and graduate into becoming regular Grameen Bank borrowers. Among the beggars are disabled, blind, retarded as well as old people with ill health. By November 2007, the cumulative membership under this program had reached 96,381.

Human Resources of Grameen Bank

There was much to appreciate about the dedication of the staff of Grameen Bank. As Mr. Mosley explained, Prof. Yunus believes that people should be adequately compensated for the work they do. They must feel that the bank is properly taking care of their families when they are out in the field from morning to evening. Hence their salaries are on par with Government salary scales. I was reminded of the MBA pass students who were picked up by a micro financing company on a salary of Rs. 70,000 pm! Would they be able to empathize with the poor?

"Stars" for Achievements

Color coded stars are bestowed to branches and Staff for 100 per cent achievement of a particular task. A branch or staff having five stars indicated the highest level of performance. The color coding is as follows:

- Green star is given for maintaining 100 per cent repayment record.
- Blue star is received for earning profit.
- Violet star for meeting all their financing out of their earned income and deposits.
- Brown star for ensuring 100% education of the children of Grameen families.
- Red star indicating branches that have succeeded in taking all its borrower's families over the poverty line.

No wonder the competition among the Grameen staff is to transform all the branches into "five star branches"!

Fig. 13.2

Impact of Grameen Bank

According to a recent survey, 64 per cent of Grameen borrowers' families have crossed the poverty line; and the remaining families are steadily progressing socially and economically. There is no legal instrument between the borrower and Grameen Bank. As Mr Barna explained, conventional banks go into the punishment mode when a borrower is taking more time in repaying the loan; as these borrowers are "defaulters". Grameen methodology allows such borrowers to reschedule their loans without making them feel that they have done anything wrong.

I found the villages brimming with life, as the poor eked out their livelihoods through income generating activities like basket weaving, fishing, tailoring, which were supplementing their farm activities. All the schemes are "very thoughtfully framed with the poor borrower in mind, who have the skill and capacity, but lack financial assistance. Even in times of disaster, Prof. Yunus gives them hope, saying at least we are alive, we will build our houses again. The Bank then stops functioning as a bank, stops taking repayments, but issues fresh loans, reschedules the existing ones till the time they are able to repay back. "Banking with the poor" is an end in itself. There are no political ambitions; only service to humanity. At the Davos Economic Summit, Dr Fakruddin Ahmed, Chief Advisor said that Bangladesh is silently ushering in social and economic changes through micro credit and other programs within the country.

About the Author

*The author is an Professor at Vaikunth Mehta National Institute of Cooperative Management, Pune.

Published in "The Administrator", Vol. No. 50, No. 1 June, 2007.

CHAPTER 14

From Banana Vendors to Wholesale Dealers

Introduction

The Cuttack Urban Cooperative Bank Ltd., is a leading Cooperative Bank in the city of Cuttack in Orissa. The Bank was setup by a group of dedicated people in the year 1981, with a mission to help the urban poor of the city.

Shri Devendranath N. Mohanty is the founder-promoter of the Bank. An advocate by profession, he was in the service of Orissa State Government as a Class-II Officer. Driven by the mission to help the needy and the poor start enterprises of their own he promoted the Cuttack Urban Cooperative Bank in Cuttack.

On January 1, 1981, the Bank was formally registered under the society Act 1956, and from September 14th in the same year, after obtaining licence from the Reserve Bank of India (RBI) it started its operations.

In the beginning, the Bank had 772 members subscribing Rs. 20/- per share. At the time of joining non-refundable entrance fee of Rs. 5/- was also charged. The Bank had an authorised share capital of Rs. 5 lakhs of which the issued share capital was Rs. 2.33 Iakhs.

The staff of the Bank comprised a Chief Executive Officer (CEO) Mr. Mohammed Tanfiqueddin, an ex-RRB employee, one cashier and four clerks.

Since the last two decades the bank has been financing the "poorest of the poor" among the urban dwellers. The urban poor run enterprises include small retail' shops, cycle shops, road side vendors, tea stall operators, fruit and vegetable vendors, artisans, pottery makers, rickshaw pullers and bamboo cane artisans.

The management chalked out a plan to help these poor people who do not get much financial assistance from the commercial banks. The exercise started with identification of business activity, motivating the poor people to start their own enterprises, completing the credit cycle of loan borrowing and its repayment as shown in the flow chart below:

The Microfinance activities financed by the Bank are illustrated in Box 1.1.

The field officers of the bank visit the "basti" and the "poorest of the poor" comprising Scheduled Castes and Scheduled tribes who live in wretched conditions in and around the city. Speaking in their local dialect, the Bank officers persuade these "assetless" poor to take a loan from the bank. Most of the Bank officers are of humble origin and are able to relate to the borrowers.

"Very often we are in the field from 8 am to 10 pm. at night" says Shri Akul Swain the Bank Manager. The amount of loan is invariably small ranging from Rs. 500 to Rs. 1000/-. They have no collateral or security to offer. Some cases of bank borrowers are illustrated below.

- ***Illustration-1:*** A rickshaw puller, who hired the rickshaw for Rs. 101/- per day was motivated by the Bank's officer to have his own rickshaw. The field officer brought him to the bank, opened a Savings Bank (SIB) account in the name of the rickshaw puller with a minimum balance of Rs. 10/-. Then, with minimum formalities was given an advance of Rs. 2000/- and handed over a new rickshaw. The rickshaw puller grew confident as a owner. He was motivated by the bank staff to pay Rs. 5/- only per day towards the loan. The field officer visited -him once a week to collect the dues. This ensured that there was no necessity for the rickshaw puller to go to the bank. Gradually the loan amount was repaid and now the rickshaw puller is free from the clutches of the owner of rickshaws from whom he used to hire rickshaw.
- ***Illustration-2*** **Banana Vendors on the Roadside:** 50 vendors in a Basti were motivated to take small loans from the bank at 12% p.a. They had obtained money from the Mahajan (moneylender) at 36% per month. 50 people took a group loan of Rs. 5000 for purchase of banana after by passing agent. The Banana vendors paid back their loan in 2 years. The daily deposit scheme had helped in ensuring quick

recovery within 3 years. Now the street side vendors are into wholesale business. They have created their own assets and purchased land. There is a positive impact on their family members also. Their children have started going to public school.

- *Illustration-3* **Silver Filigree-Workers:** Orissa is World famous for its filigree work—The Bank officers identified the basti of Goldsmith families. This is a family business handed down over generations for the past 1000 years. Families goldsmiths were motivated to take loans individually. They started with Rs. 10,000 and now the loan amount has increased to Rs. 10 lakhs. Earlier they were doing the work in their own house. Now they have a workshop and also a show room
- *Illustration-4* **Bamboo Cane Workers:** Members from a Scheduled Caste were given a loan of Rs. 3000 per head. The Bank officers had interactions with them and persuaded them to open an account with Rs. 10/- with minimum formalities. The women borrowers made gudis (baskets), khas khas curtain, partition, bucket-token (basket), sofa, mattress etc.

Likewise the bank started financing the urban poor and gradually gained their confidence. Now it is acclaimed as "People's Bank". The urban poor now believe that it is their bank. They created their assets with the help of the bank and now they are in a position to avail bigger loan amounts from the bank. In view of the past record of the borrowers, the bank is confident of recovery. The Bank is guided by six principles in its functioning. It has helped around 30,000 people with a loan amount amount of Rs. 60 crores. Many borrowers who initially borrowed Rs. 10,000/- are now able to avail a loan of Rs. 10 lakhs. In the process they have expanded their business and created some assets. The bank has emerged as the bank with the largest number of transactions among 50 bank branches in Cuttack town. Each month the Bank sanctions loans to nearly 200 small borrowers starting with loans of Rs. 25,000 to Rs. 50,000.

Daily Collection System

Daily Collection System plays a vital role in the recovery of microfinance. The system is simple and involves the following activities.

1. Everyday the agent collects from loanee Rs. 2/- to Rs. 10/-.

2. Daily receipt is given to the loanee.
3. At the end of the month, a balance confirmation letter with the signature of bank officers/manager is issued to loanee.
4. Daily collections of agent are transferred to suspense account in the name of the agent.
5. At the end of the month amount is transferred from the suspense account to "5anchayeeta Deposit Account" of the depositor. In this way field agents cover almost 50,000 customers. Every agent has 200–500 customers. The field agents are given 3% of collected amount as commission.

Recovery Staff: Duties

1. The staff covers 20 persons in a day for recovery and enquiry of new proposals. The recommendation of the recovery staff is final. A Review Meeting is held every fortnight at the Branch and every month at the Head office in the presence of Board Members.
2. The field officers maintain a "Field Diary" listing the visits to each beneficiary, the loans given, the recovery date etc. The diary is checked by the Branch Manager once a week. To ensure prompt recovery the field officers visit the borrower on the day he has promised to make the repayment. In case the borrower is not able to keep his word, he is asked to repay by the next date. The field officer marks the date in his diary and visits the borrower again on the fixed day. The borrower is persuaded to repay. Most often the loan is repayed by the fourth visit. If not, "request letter" with white color code is issued. If the request letter fails to elicit a response, a demand letter with yellow code is sent. The third warning bears a "red color code" which is also given to guarantors. The "legal notice" is given only as a last resort.

Observations Based on Bank's Experience

1. Poor people who have small business in urban areas are bankable.
2. Saving of the poor need to be tapped on daily basis,
3. Cooperative banks are better predisposed than commercial banks in microfinancing.

4. Methods of keeping accounts and. financial records should be simple.
5. Sensitization of bankers towards microfinance is essential for the success of such interventions.
6. Introduction of computer and reduction of manual tasks will prove to be cost effective.
7. Use of non-conventional energy and technology can widen the scope of microenterprises in urban and semi-urban areas.
8. Expenses incurred by the bank on imparting training/capacity building for the project beneficiaries may be supported by Development Financial Institutions.

Conclusion

The small borrowers are the main clients of the bank. On the annual day. 32 small borrowers were felicitated and awarded prizes by the bank. It is their entrepreneurial spirit that will keep the Bank alive. True to their motto of "Sewa and Vikas" the bank plans to bring all the urban poor within its fold. 50 far the Bank was lending to individual borrowers. The bank now wants to form SHGs and facilitate group intermediation as an effective tool to inculcate thrift and saving habit among the local population.

CHAPTER 15

The Mojari Experience

Rajasthan Crafts history and have a centuries old history and have evolved over the years. These crafts like terracotta, blue pottery, leather mojari, namdha, durries, jewellery, woodcrafts, metal crafts, stones, sand stone, and paintings were originally objects of daily life for the people of Rajasthan. They adorned almost everything from the walls of their houses, to their clothes and their footwear. Yet all these traditional skills of yore are today dying as units shut down and artisans are forced to migrate to the cities and live in conditions of pecuniary and drudgery. Moreover, the country's economic policies of liberalization, privatization and globalization create problems of marketing the artisan's produce.

In 1995 the Swiss Development Corporation (SDC), Government of India (GOI) and the National Bank for Agriculture and Rural Development (NABARD) conducted a study to examine the potential of Non-Farm Sector (NFS). This study was conducted in 8 states. Consequently the Rajasthan Government framed a NFS policy and RUDA was set up as an "exclusive agency to promote rural microenterprise in the state". It's the only one of its kind of the country.

Published in "Yojana", Vol. 49, February, 2005.

- RUDA (Rural Non-Farm Development Agency) is registered under the Societies Registration Act.
- Its primary mandate is to:
  (a) Create alternate avenues of employment
  (b) Generate incremental income
- Over the last 7 years, RUDA has evolved as an innovative, creative and a highly professional agency.

RUDA is perhaps the only agency of its kind promoting rural micro-enterprises on sub-sectoral basis. Initially, 3 sub-sectors viz. leather, wool

& minor-minerals (stone, ceramics and pottery) were identified. During the 10th Five Year Plan three new sub-sectors namely Handicrafts, Khadi & Village Industries and Handlooms have been added. RUDA works through a cluster based approach. It adopts a truly integrated strategy to promote the sector and all its interventions are based on the felt needs of the producers.

RUDA's Package of Interventions Include

- Sub-sectoral analysis
- Capacity audit of artisan clusters
- Identifying ruling constraints
- Organizing artisans
- Providing skill training/upgradation
- Technology dissemination
- Product development and design support
- Credit facilitation
- Market facilitation.

Operation *Mojari*

To take a first look at the Ruda Interventions, I visited the Mojari cluster groups at Udaipuria about 35 kms from Jaipur. This nondescript village is off the Sikar Road, National Highway 11 to Bikaner. As you drive the dusty road you find camel carts passing at frequent intervals. The land is dry and barren making it unsuitable for agriculture. With a population of 5,000 these people have traditionally been cobblers. But with modernization and factory made footwear, the ethnic "mojaris" were fast becoming a dying art.

In 1995 UNDP initiated a National Level Development Programme (NLDP) for technical upgradation of the traditional footwear of Rajasthan. Five districts were selected viz. Nagor, Jaipur, Jodhpur, Pali and Jalore.

The RUDA team of professionals who had completed a two-year advanced diploma course from the Central Footwear Training Institute, Agra visited these hamlets and met its denizens. Initially there was a lot of resistance to change.

A scientific examination of the footwear revealed that it was not technically sound. Firstly the fitting was poor because of faulty size measurements. Size was generally measured by the hand ("unglion se napte"). Hence there was no standardization of size and fittings. RUDA then introduced the standardized British System.

Secondly, the shoe mould ("farma") was made of wood, which used to change with the changing weather. The wood would expand in summer and contract in rainy or winter days. RUDA introduced "polymer moulds" which were lighter accurate and not malleable by the weather. I saw the three! in one yellow colored moulds consisting of the front, middle and rear parts strung by a rope with a nail passing through the middle to keep its balance.

Thirdly, and more importantly, there was no distinction between the left and right footwear. Which often lead to stress for the wearer. The new "mojari" has made foot comfortable for its left right foot distinction, standard sizing and fittings. The back seam was stitched by hand, and hence was painful. To provide more comfort to the wearer, the stitching was changed.

RUDA innovated on new designs in different textures like satin, velvet and jute. This expanded the markets for mojaris in the domestic and international markets. Mojaris were very popular with the Japanese as well. RUDA prepared a colorful catalogue of the patterns in embroidery, punch, applique and weave. These were distributed in villages for the artisans.

RUDA in a big way promoted these *mojaris* through fairs, buyer and seller meets. Their marketing department through better pricing helped get higher margins to the artisans. Where earlier a pair of *mojaris* would fetch about Rs. 135–150, could now fetch Rs. 400–500; an increase of 230%.

Community Mobilization

Initially SHG mobilizing was difficult, but then, 45 groups were formed with 10 members. I interacted with two such groups at Udaipuria. They belonged to the same extended family. In a typical assembly line manufacturing, each person was working on one of the operations in sequence-pattern cutting on leader board/paper, chiseling the lower and upper sole, hammering and pasting the foam in between for softness and comfort, stitching the attachments of the sole and the upper side. Then the finishing would be done on the machine dye and dry the mojaris on the charpoy in the sun. On an average, the artisans were finishing 25 mojaris per day.

The group made 150 *mojaries* per week and earned Rs. 30,000 per month. Earlier, working individually, required two days to finish one *mojaris.* Each artisan earned only about Rs. 400 per month. RUDA intervention resulted in increase in productivity and of more than 10% in income.

One worker said "we were first working in makeshift tents, now we have pucca workplaces". I could see bricks laid for a pucca house, which would be built very soon. He told me he had three children. The children were studying in school.

The once dying art has given life to the cobblers of Udaipuria.

The RUDA experience has provided valuable insights into the process of decentralization and management of rural enterprises through community participation. The road ahead for RUDA is envisaged as:

- Programme formulation
- Networking
- Upgradation and modernization of facilties.
- Capacity building and training

The salient features of the RUDA model are:

(a) Training is carried to the door (village) of the potential training target group.
(b) Training generates employment and income generation in rural non-farm sector.
(c) Spread of economic activity among the marginal people.
(d) It is a win-win situation to both the trainees and the implementing agency.

The success of the programme has been due to:

- Providing alternative source of income of artisans.
- Poverty alleviation while addressing local skills.
- It ensures equitable participation of marginalized groups.
- By ensuring community participation, the programme elicits public support and taps the traditional skills of community.

The RUDA approach has facilitated the progress towards alternate avenues for employment particularly non-farm avenues. Through RUDA is government sponsored, it is not governmentalized. It thus provides stability with flexibility.

The UNDP-NLDP sponsored project wound up in March 2002. However, the Udaipura artisans have a long way to go, on the road to sustainable development.

One suggestion was that the groups could be registered as cooperatives. This would facilitate the group to have credit linkages with banks. Secondly, a Common Facility Center (CFC) would help the group procure machines such as stitching and furnishing machine, leather compressing machine, fly wheel and dye cutting machine. Third there was an idea of a raw material bank. Last but not least promotion of leader tanneries.

RUDA is emerging as a media and documentation center to educate and train artisans. The website of RUDA would catalogue all its products and push its wares internationally.

CHAPTER 16

Gender Sensitisation in Cooperatives

(A Case of a Cooperative Dairy)

History of the Organisation

Kolhapur Zilla Sahakari Dudh Utpadak Sangh Ltd. (Gokul Dairy), is a cooperative dairy set up on 16th March, 1963. Fifteen years later in 1978, the National Dairy Development Board included "Gokul" under its food programme operations. This triggered the commissioning of a full fledged dairy plant at Gokul Shirgaon, Kolhapur in 1985 and subsequently four chilling centres at Tawarewadi, Gogave, Gadhinglaj and Bidri. The installed capacity of the main dairy plant and the chilling centers is given in the Table 16.1 below.

Table 16.1: Milk Handling Capacities

	Lakh Liters.
Main Dairy Plant at Kolhapur	7.00
Chilling Center at Linganur	1.25
Chilling Center at Boravade	1.00
Chilling Center at Tavarewadi	1.00
Chilling Center at Gogave	0.50

*Awarded FIRST prize in All India Case Writing Competition by Indian Institute of Public Administration (IIPA), New Delhi.

At present, Gokul is procuring about 6 lakh litres of milk per day, from about 5 lakh 40 thousand men and women milk producers in the district.

Table 16.2

Area of Operation	*Kolhapur District*
No. of societies supplying milk	3,452
No. of member societies	3,011
No. of villages in the district	1,230
No. of villages covered	1190
No. of farmer members	5.40 lakhs

Objectives

1. Its primary objective is development of infrastructure for the procurement of milk in rural areas, to ensure an assured market for milk producers at the best remunerative prices throughout the year.
2. To provide quality milk and milk products to fulfill the growing needs the consumers in Maharashtra at affordable prices.
3. To organize the co-operative dairy societies of milk producers at the village level.
4. To supplement the programme extension and inputs, with particular reference to feed and fodder production and implement an intensive breeding programme for milch animals whereby milk production can be increased.
5. Imparting training for developing human resource at rural level for effective leadership, management skills and improvement of services to rural milk producers.

Gokul's Key Strength

(a) *Milk Procurement*

Gokul has always set a landmark and exemplary standards for milk procurement for Quality.

Consider the year 1985, when the average milk procurement was 1.15 lac ltrs. per day with 676 village level societies affiliated to the Dudhsangh. Since then, the figure has shot up year after year. In 2000, the average and peak procurement was 4.50 and 5.27 lac ltrs. per day respectively. Presently it is 5.40 lac ltrs. per day. Figures show an astonishing 3% raise in milk procurement as compared to last year.

It is really commendable as the rated capacity of the dairy is only 7.0 lakh ltrs. per day. All this milk is collected from about 3450 village level dairy co-operatives on 197 milk routes.

Table 16.3: Milk Procurement: (2005–06)

Annual Milk Procurements (Liters)	19.09 Crores.
Total Milk Handling (Own + Outside) (Liters.)	20.50 Crores
Total Milk Collection Routes.	197 Nos.
Average Milk Procurement (LPD)	5,23,000
Average Buffalo Milk Procurement (LPD)	3,50,000
Average Cow Milk Procurement (LPD)	1,73,000
Peal Procurement (LPD)	6,38,000
Lean Procurement (LPD)	4,12,000
Total Sourage of Milk (%)	0.13%

(b) *Developing a Global Market*

The Dudhsangh's products are very popular in the market. Marketed under the brand name "Gokul", they include White Butter, Table Butter, Shrikhand, Mango Shrikhand and Ghee. Lassi & Paneer are two more delights which have been launched recently. Dahi, Butter Milk & Sterilized Flavoured Milk are in the pipeline. Taking a Step in international marketing. Gokul has started exporting to Sri Lanka Skimmed Milk Powder. This shows the Sangh's presence in the global market.

(c) *Environmental Challenges and Innovations*

Gokul Dairy is always looking for employing new methods that are efficient as well as cost-effective. In order to minimize the consumption of water, recycling the treated water obtained from Effluent Treatment Plant has been planned. Even the lush green gardens and landscapes developed at Gokul's Head Quarters have been maintained on drip irrigation system, where again recycled water is used. Talking more about energy conservation, Gokul Dairy processes 160–170 ltrs. of milk, as against the industrial average of 115 ltrs. Similarly, to process 32 ltrs. of milk 1 unit of electricity is consumed, whereas the industrial average figure is 28 litrs.

(d) *Spreading Out*

Beginning 1988, liquid milk marketing was launched in Mumbai by the Dudhsangh. Sales initially were 16,000 LPD. Today to meet the requirements of different customers four different varieties of milk, viz. Classic (Buffalo) milk, Cow Milk, Tonned Milk and Double Tonned Milk are marketed in Mumbai which account for more than 3,50,000 LPD. The same has also its strong market presence in Pune, Kolhapur and other parts of Western/Southern Maharashtra with a total consumption of 1,10,000 LPD. These varieties meet the different fat requirements of the customer and at the same time they are effectively priced to suit each one's pocket. In addition, to fulfill the constitutional obligation, milk through tankers is supplied to the State Federation as per their requirement.

Cattle Feed Plant

In the year 1982, Dudhsangh started the production of 100 MT cattle feed to meet nutritional requirement of the animals. This has now been expanded to 200 MT per day. The production, later switched to by-pass feed to meet more demand. The Cattle Feed is marketed under the brand 'Mahalaxmi'.

Dudhsangh will soon have a new by-pass protein feed and mineral mixture plant to meet the demand of Milk producers. Looking at the growing demand of Cattle Feed, construction of new Cattle Feed Plant with 300 MT per day capacity is under planning.

Technical Input Activities

A team of 45 trained veterinary graduates operating from 33 different locations in the district are catering to the preventive and clinical veterinary needs of the dairy farmers. Each veterinarian looks after about 15–20 villages and provides these services round the clock at the farmers doorsteps.

Breeding Services

In its operational area 240 artificial Insemination centers have been established by the union. All the necessary inputs to these centers such as liquid nitrogen, semen, sheath, and even cryogenic containers are made available by the union.

Dudhsangh has entered into an agreement with National Dairy Development Board and is implementing "Dairy Herd Improvement Programme Action" (DIPA) in order to improve the genetic material of the female animals to improve their productivity.

Fodder Development

Availability of sufficient quantity of good and nutritious fodder is an essential prerequisite for sustained milk production. In view of this a team of 4 agricultural graduates with the assistance of 5 supervisors are working under fodder development section of the union. Under this program seeds of improved fodder varieties are distributed at 25% subsidized cost. Besides manual chaff cutters and power driven chaff cutters are distributed at 25% & 30% subsidy respectively. About 100 tones of fodder seed are distributed annually.

Benefit to the Members

Milk Producers are the pillars of the Dudh Sangh. Hence the Sangh has planned its activities which are 'Milk Producer Oriented'. The milk producers enjoy the following benefits.

- Year round market for the surplus milk is available.
- Remunerative milk price based on its quality.
- Technical input program for increasing milk production.
- Loan and advance guarantee for purchase of dairy equipments, implements and dairy animals.
- Employment opportunities for urban and rural population.

Organizational Reward System

This is the only "One of its Kind" Scheme introduced by the Dudhsangh in the entire country. In order to take care of the milk producers in their old age, Dudhsangh has introduced a Novel Provident Fund Scheme. Under the Scheme, for every litre of milk collected by the Dudhsangh, 10 paise per litre would be contributed by the Milk Producer, 10 paise per litre by village level Dairy Co-operative and 10 paise per litre by Dudhsangh, making a total contribution of 30 paise per litre. The money would be kept in separate account by the Dudhsangh. The Milk Producer, after attaining the age of 60 years, can withdraw the amount accumulated in her/his account. The scheme would give financial security to the Milk Producers and would come handy at the old age.

Quality Management and ISO 9001:9002

In order to improve the quality of the plant and its output Gokul implemented a quality management system. Gokul has to it's credit certification of being an IS/ISO: 9001:2000 & IS: 15000:1998, Quality Management, Food Safety System & HACCP Certified dairy. The unit is also accredited by Export inspection council. These quality standards will help Gokul in competing at international levels.

Human Resources

Gokul has a dedicated staff of human resources comprising of almost 1939 people spread across its Headquarter, chilling centers and Mumbai Office. Among them are 5 ladies who are spearheading the women Dairy Co-operatives and Gokul Gram Vikas Yojana activities.

Gokul Gram Vikas Yojana

Women are the mainstay of the dairy industry. It is important that women who take care of the cattle and milk the cow, get remunerative prices, for the milk and are actively involved in decision making with this in mind in 1990, the Gokul Gram Vikas Yojana and Women's Leadership Development Program was started in 1995, Women SHGs were formed for the economic development. At present there are 750 SHGs, having a savings corpus of 90 lakhs, and loaning of Rs. 1 crore 50 lakh (Annexure-1). The groups are functioning smoothly with a recovery of 100%. There have been no instances where the loans have not been repaid. Moreover, it has strengthened the social ties in villages. They have been able to curb anti social behavior such as drinking, settling family disputes, health awareness, cultural programs.

Insights from SHG Members

The "intangible" benefits that were achieved were visible during the experiences shared by SHG representatives. The following cases highlights the benefits.

1. Social mobilization of women in villages. It is an opportunity for women to come together and interact amongst themselves irrespective of age, or education. It was observed that in the SHGs there are both elderly women along with the younger. The younger women are educated upto 10th Std. In such groups, it is these women who keep the accounts and look for growth and further prospects of SHGs.
2. Another quality of SHG is that it has given the women in the village "a face" and an identity of her own. As one of the members narrated that women in the village hardly came out of her house; but now she is able to go to the Bank, the collector's office and stand for election. She has become a "visible" face in the village.
3. On the other hand the male dominance is no longer restricting women. There is a gradual change in the attitudes of men; as they realize that women in a group can be heard more loudly than than a single women. It was refreshing to hear that women of some groups left their domestic care for a while and undertook a sight seeing trip to near by pilgrim centers.
4. The SHG process has emboldened the women to take decisions. For example a woman member shared her feelings of how in the face of resistance from her mother-in-law and husband; she decided to grow some vegetables in the garden to supplement the family income. She narrated how she dug the soil, went to the market to get quality seeds and was ultimately successful in growing vegetables.
5. The internal loaning has equipped her with skills of accounting and book keeping, opening savings account, depositing and withdrawing money from bank, utilizing money for business. The Group Secretary is taught to keep the ledger and note down the monthly deposits, and loans advanced to women. Women generally borrow for medical or educational needs of their children, or to buy income producing assets like sewing machines. One of the group members has a cable business helping her to earn commission of 2%.
6. Women are economically empowered. A woman member proudly said that she no longer has to spread her hands in front of her husband for money; in fact now it is the husband who ask them for money!

7. Women are enthusiastic to take part in cultural programme on occasions such as independence day and festival occasions such as Ganeshotsav, Dussera, Diwali, rangoli competitions.
8. Some members of SHGs, have taken to income generating activities. They are preparing traditional Maharashtrian food items like Nachani Papad, Kurdai, Sandge. This group members took training conducted by Swayam Siddh Yojana and have been able to make quality products that have demand in cities. They sell these items under the Gokul" brand name. They were ready to train other group members also. Other business activities taken up were bakery, tailoring, Nirma, patrawali.
9. The SHGs have generated social awareness as some have been actively able to settle domestic problems faced by women, anti-liquour, cleanliness.
10. The SHGs took active part in helping the flood affected victims by distributing food items, clothes etc.
11. An amazing quality of women were their creative ability to sing and make couplets on SHGs.
12. As SHGs become successful existing SHGs members help women from near by village to form SHGs in their own areas. It thus has a multiplier effect.

Gender Sensitization

Gokul is committed to spreading rural progress and prosperity. Although the women take care of cattle and milk the cow, her work remains "invisible". Through it's Gokul Gram Vikas Yojana, women's education and training, leadership development, SHG and microenterprise development and Women Dairy Cooperatives (WDCs) are being promoted. However, this program can be successful only if there is a proactive role of men. The management of Gokul felt that there was a strong need for Gender Sensitization among the Gokul Union Staff supervisors, field officers, training officers women mobilizes and and the Chairman of Cooperative Dairy. They took the decision to approach the Vaikunth Mehta National Institute of Cooperative Management, an apex Institute based in Pune to conduct these workshops.

Perceptions from the Gender Sensitization Workshop

Formation and Membership of Dairy Cooperative Societies (DCS)

The byelaws of the dairy society allow women to become members, nevertheless male membership is more. To encourage women to be members, the mobilizers of Gokul hold discussions with Management Committees members or leaders. However, it was felt that when women become members, they should be made aware of their duties under the byelaws. In forming cooperatives, women take the help and advice of men. Gokul has organized 681 Women Dairy Cooperatives (WDCS) in the district.

Table 16.4: Details of Women Dairy Project (As on 31.03.2006)

The Programme Started from	*1995*
No. of Villages Covered	276
No. of DCS Covered	681
No. of Programmes Organized	4185
No. of Participants	1,51,203

The author conducted a "Gender Sensitization Workshop" (20th to 24th February, 2006) for Gokul Union Staff, Supervisors, field officers, training officers, women mobilizers as well as Chairman/Chairperson, Directors.

Representation of Board of Management

The legislation of 331/3 representation of women on the Board has opened the doors in a big way for women participation as Directors on the Board. The Government of Maharashtra, was one of the first states in India which amended the Cooperatives Societies Act by introducing a compulsory provision of 30% representation of women on the Board of Directors. This will enable women to be a part of the decision making process.

The 1992 amendment of the Maharashtra Cooperatives Societies Act introduced reservation of seats on committees of societies for women members. Under section 73B, committee of each society will have representation of women members as follows:

(a) One seat on the committee consisting of not more than 9 committee members.

(b) Two seats on the committee consisting of 10 or more, but not exceeding 19 committee members.

(c) Three seats on the committee of 20 or more committee members accordingly, as per the directives Gokul has 2 women Directors on the Board of 16 committee members.

Jobs Held by Female Employees in Dairy Cooperatives

Women are found in the lower levels of the job hierarchy. These include Typing, clerical, computer, telephone operator, laboratory technician, peon, extension activity. It appears there is much scope for women in middle and senior level management.

Society Meetings

It was observed that meetings are held at times which are not convenient to women. As also there are no facilities like crèche available. Hence it is very necessary that the meetings are held as per the convenient time for women. It must also take into consideration her personal convenience. Similarly, in some cases the notice for the meeting is not given to women. However men are informed of it. It was felt that women need to be more alert about the meeting schedules.

Election and Voting

Although women have the right to vote, she does not exercise her independent thinking. The men in the house determine whom to give vote. This appeared to be very challenging for women who, now had the opportunity to think on their own.

Participation of Women in Decision Making Process

Very few women are present in the Management Committee Meetings. In the absence of the women, her male representative takes part in the decision making. Thus the participation of women in the decision making process is less. At the time of voting, women toe the lines of their husband. Women do not decide for themselves. This may have to do with years of social conditioning of being subservient to men. It was strongly felt that women should gain confidence and be emboldened to take decisions and protect her interests. So also in economic matters, women are not informed. Hence there is much need for training and personality development excercises.

Position of Women in Dairy Cooperative Societies (DCS)

The participation of women in mainstream or marginal activities were identified as follows (Table 16.5).

Table 16.5

Mainstream Activities	*Female*	*Male*	*Marginal Activities*	*Female*	*Male*
Formation of Dairy Cooperatives	N	Y	Milk collection	Y	Y
Membership in Primary Societies	Y	Y	Festive Programmes (Haldikumkum Program etc.)	Y	N
Participation in General Meeting	N	Y	Bill payment		Y
Extraordinary Meeting	N	Y	Training		Y
Monthly Meetings	N	Y			
Participation in election process	N	Y			
Voting rights		Y			
Training		Y			
Distribution		Y			

Access to Resources

Training and Education

Women cannot assume leadership role unless they have had an access to education and training programs. On a positive note, it was found that 75% women do participate in these programs. In designing training programs women's needs and potentials were considered. These programs were also easily accessible to women as they were fixed only after taking into consideration the place, day and time which were suitable to women. Care was also taken that there were no festivals during the time, which would make it difficult for women to attend the programs

Extension Services, Technical Expertise Production Inputs

Women are in equal proportion to men as milk producers. Women have access to modern methods, clean milk production etc. These services are also available to female headed households.

Credit and Loan Facilities

Women experience problems in acquiring bank loans and credit because:

1. No land is in her name
2. Women lack education and training
3. Patriarcial society or male dominance.

Hence it is very necessary to give equal rights to women; provide her education and training, and she must inculcate the saving habit. Gokul is actively promoting women's thrift societies to encourage women to save.

Table 16.6: Details on Women Thrift Cooperatives (As on 31.03.2006)

No. of Thrift Cooperatives	900
No. of Villages Covered	276
No. of Participating Members	17,368
Total Funds Collected (Lakh Rs.)	142
Loans Advanced (Lakh Rs.)	165
Loans Outstanding (Lakh Rs.)	70

Market Outlets and Transport Facilities Marketing. Opportunities should be made available to women. For this "Gokul" has already initiated action for providing marketing outlets, stalls, etc for the purpose.

Problems

The following obstacles were perceived in women's participation:

- There is no proper evaluation of the capability of a woman. Hence it is important to make the women aware of their own potential and her talent. For this to happen she may have to be freed from some of her household duties and be given freedom.
- To some extent men give less recognition or value to women's work.

- Hindrances created by Cooperative. Act of the State:

  Unlike other States of the country, the Cooperative. Act of Maharashtra has a provision for formation of more than one Milk Cooperative at the Village level. Because of this, in almost all the villages in the area of a Milk Union, more than one milk Cooperative is in operation. Many of the villages have 4, 5, even up to 10 Milk Cooperatives!

  The Maharashtra State Cooperative. Act has a provision under which, for registering a Milk Society under general category, minimum 250 Liters of milk is to be collected daily. However, to register a Women Cooperative., the quantity of milk needs to be only 50 Liters a day. But since, most of the villages have more than one Milk Cooperative, the quantity of milk gets divided and as such many times, it becomes rather difficult to register exclusive Women Cooperatives in a village.
- ***Political Intrigues:*** As mentioned above, because of lacuna in the Cooperatives Act, various politically interested Milk Producers try to organize a separate Milk Cooperatives. While enacting the law, the whole idea was that the village, where milk is available in large quantity, or if it is difficult for the producers to travel a long distance to supply the milk, Dairy Cooperatives. were formed at the village level.. However, in order to get more members and in turn get more voters, it is observed that decision to form more Milk Cooperatives. are taken to benefit the interest of political parties rather than benefit the Milk producers. Because of this, the Milk Unions also has to incur additional expenditure on monitoring and coordinating various technical inputs activities.
- Low educational or technical levels of women hinders their growth and progress.

Economic Empowerment, Equality and Gender Awareness

For the economic empowerment of women Gokul has made special efforts to:

- Give the milk bill to women only
- Personality development programs are conducted
- Formation of Self Help Groups
- Gokul management gives help to women societies
- Rs. 15/- per head for visit to Dairy.

Measures taken to support Gender Equality and Gender Awareness are as follows:

- Training and exposure visits to other successful dairy, for example Anand, Gujarat
- Training programs in dairy business and personality development
- Women leadership programs.

Impact of Gender Sensitization Training

The participants were able to share their experiences and express their views and attitude on gender issues. Most of the trainees had put in 25–30 years of service with Gokul, but were attending a Gender Sensitization programme for the first time.

The training was able to bring about an awareness of gender issues. An understanding of these issues helped in preparing an Action Plan as follows:

1. The Chairman of Kolindre, Pernoli decided to increase women members in their dairies by 10% and 100% respectively. Similarly, the Chairman from Mahagond said he would endeavour to associate 10 women as members.
2. They also agreed to motivate women to actively participate in meetings and decision making. Smt. Mali from Pimple said she would personally attend the meetings of DCS, so that other women also in her village could follow her.
3. The Chairman of Dairy Society (DCS) from Ingle said he would recruit women as employees and staff.
4. Almost all were unanimous that women will be taken on the committee and as employees.
5. All Women Directors reached a consensus that they will actively participate in meetings.
6. The Chairperson from Bhadgaon, Hasoor Compu said that their DCS will participate in forming SHGs with active involvement of women.
7. All the trainees were unanimous that they wanted to spread awareness on Gender Sensitization through training.

Learning Lessons

1. Cooperatives are voluntary organizations, based on the principle of equality, open and democratic membership. Nevertheless, it is observed that all though cooperatives laws and bye-laws do not discriminate; gender inequity in cooperatives does exit. For example, male heads of households become cooperative members even if it is the women who provide a major part of the labor input in dairy. Women should be actively involved as members of the cooperatives If the participation of women is increased in this way, such an approach would lead to a sustainable cooperative development.
2. As compared to the total number of cooperatives, the number of women cooperatives is still small, Exclusive women cooperative constitute only 2.1% of the total number of cooperatives. The Cooperatives Act can be amended to encourage formation of Women Cooperatives.
3. A few successful dairy cooperatives like Gokul, have created a revolution of sorts by forming exclusive Women Dairy Cooperative Societies (WDCS). They have economically empowered women by making the bill in her name and giving payment to women. Women Dairy Societies (WDCs) can be replicated on the lines of the success of Gokul.
4. It is critically important to conduct gender sensitization workshops to all personnel in Cooperatives; including members, employees, leaders and Cooperators

The author conducted a "Gender Sensitization Workshop" (20th to 24th February, 2006) for Gokul Union Staff, Supervisors, field officers, training officers, women mobilizers as well as Chairman/Chairperson, Directors.

The Author was awarded the FIRST prize in case study writing competition conducted by Indian Institute of Public Administration, New Delhi.

Chapter 17

From Margin to Mainstream—Empowering Women in Cooperatives

Sustainable development goals (SDGs) have been among the most crucial recent developments. Inclusion and equity are prominently at the central stage of many SDGs. "Leave no one behind" is the foundational principle of the United Nations' Agenda 2030.

THE lives of people in poor countries will improve faster in the next 15 years than at any other time in history. And their lives will improve more than anyone else's." So predict Bill and Melinda Gates in their annual letter, published on January 22nd. They hope the SDGs will continue the good work of the MDGs. It is an empowering force that we know of.

For the goals to be reached, everyone needs to do their part: governments, the private sector, civil society and people. The SDGs recognize cooperative enterprises as important players within the private sector to achieve the goals. Cooperatives are the most effective enabling, equalizing and empowering force. The United Nations declared the International Cooperative Year (ICY) 2012 with the realization that "cooperatives make a better world".

Cooperatives have emerged as socio-economic organizations that would bring equality in incomes.

As Ban Ki-Moon the then UN Secretary General had said that Co-operatives are a reminder to the international community that it is possible to pursue both economic viability and social responsibility.

Cooperatives in India—Highlights

- India is ranked 6th in terms of number of cooperatives.
- 72.2% of population live in 6,38,000 villages.

- Number of cooperatives at all levels are 6,10,020.
- Membership of 263.6 million.

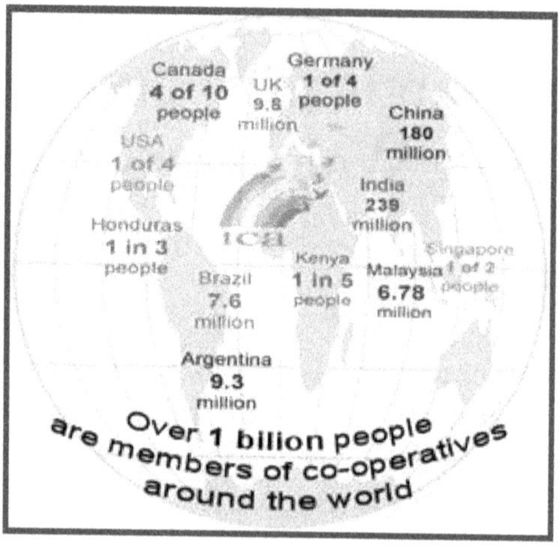

- At a time when income inequality is rising around the world, the Cooperative Model is a solution for the inequality. Its Principles and Values set it apart from all other forms of entrepreneurial organizations. Those principles state that membership in a cooperative is open without discrimination to all people. Open membership affords, access to wealth creation and poverty elimination.

It is now four decades that the United Nations helped focus public attention on the important role women can play in socio economic development. From Mexico to Copenhagen and Nairobi to finally Beijing has brought centre stage these issues. They are further enhanced by the Beijing Platform for Action, the MDGs and the SDGs.

India is a signatory to Convention on the Elimination of all forms of Discrimination against Women. (CEDAW)

The report of the National Commission of Self Employed Women and women in the Informal sector expresses that "cooperative is an important instrument through which women can get access to credit, production inputs, marketing facilities and other forms of support." Women are organized in their economic activities and their produce is sold for a remunerative price. This can be facilitated through women cooperatives. Cooperatives provide a forum for women to come together and acquire better bargaining power.

- Women are active in most types of cooperatives such as banks, dairy, consumers, agricultural marketing, fisheries and allied activities, thrift and credit societies, producer societies and industrial cooperatives yet as compared to the total number of cooperatives, the number of women cooperatives is still small. Exclusive women cooperatives constitute only 1.7% of the total number of cooperative
- Strategies for Mainstreaming Women in Cooperatives.

It is therefore, necessary to work out a strategy to bring women in the mainstream of the cooperative movement.

The strategy has three components :

- Integration of women in cooperatives through participation of women in leadership and decision making bodies.

Economic empowerment of women through development of entrepreneurship, microfinance and Mitigation of discrimination and bias against women 97th Constitutional Amendment.

- The Amendment gives the Right to every citizen to form cooperative societies and

  Provide for cooperative education and training for its members

  However the challenge is to

  Sensitizing management to cooperative values and principals

  Ensuring the competitiveness of cooperatives

  Develop human resource capacities

  Form women cooperatives and/women dairy cooperatives (WDCS).

Invisible Women; Women in Leadership

Women remain invisible. Women leaders in cooperatives are few or none. There is very meager presence of women in committees. In top management level women comprise hardly 17.65, 4.3% and 3.2% in three apex level cooperative institutions viz. National Cooperative Union of India (NCUI), National Agricultural Cooperative Marketing Federation NAFED) & National Consumer Cooperative Federation NCCF). The very less representation of women in the Board of Committee levels shows that women have no significant role in the decision-making policies of these federations.

If we look deeper into the qualitative participation of women i.e. their involvement in elections, decision-making about cooperative activities and financial matters, women representation is negligible; in the ratio of 1:40.

Quantitative and Qualitative Participation

Some notable findings that emerged from a workshop on Gender Integration in Cooperatives were.

The participation of women is more in middle management than senior management.

Women have not been represented on elected bodies or in top management in numbers proportionate to their contribution.

Women have no significant role in the decision making policies of these federations.

Because of the above-mentioned points, the qualitative participation of women in cooperatives leaves much to be desired Therefore, there is not much headway in the involvement of more women in cooperatives. As a result, the cooperative movement has lost the benefit of additional human resources which women cooperators could provide in the successful promotion of social and economic objectives Men and women serving as elected representatives are accountable to the membership in primaries; and members have equal voting rights. It is hence necessary to develop Leadership Development programs.

Good Pratice Policy Initiatives

To involve women in the decision making processes, the Government of India introduced the 73rd and 74th Amendment, encouraging women in local bodies of self government—-Panchayat Raj.

Empowerment of Women through Cooperatives in Maharashtra

The Government of Maharashtra, was one of the first state in India which amended the Cooperative Societies Act by introducing a compulsory provision of 30% representation of women on the Board of Directors. This will enable the women to be a part of the decision-making process.

Women Representation on Boards

The 1992 amendment of the Maharashtra Cooperative Societies Act introduced reservation of seats on committees of societies for women members.

Under section 73B, committee of each society will have representation of women members as follows:

- One seat on the committee consisting of not more than 9 committee members.
- Two seats on the committee consisting of 10 or more, but not exceeding 19 committee members.
- Three seats on the committee of 20 or more committee members.

The participants at a National Seminar sought to "Empower" women through strategies and an Action Plan that enumerated the following:

- Supporting women's organizations, formal and informal, to develop self-employment and entrepreneurship among women.
- Working with organizations to build awareness and ensure their participation in programs for women.

AND in pursuance of the broad objectives:

- To develop micro-credit systems for women entrepreneurs.
- To develop best practices in financial services to women entrepreneurs.
- Improve data collection on women micro entrepreneurs and enterprise.
- To conduct impact studies of support programs including credit to develop women entrepreneurship.

Good Practise in Cooperative Banks

Kallappanna Aawade Ichalkaranji Janata Sahakari Bank, Ichalkaranji, Kolhapur, Maharashtra, India Kallappanna Aawade Ichalkaranji Janata Sahakari Bank is a leading bank of South Western Maharashtra. It has a network of 45 computerized branches spread across Maharashtra and Karnataka state. Its uniqueness is that it has linked formal banking with informal groups. It has a Microfinance division to oversee the microfinance operations. It has animators that facilitate mobilizing women into Self Help Groups. They urge the members to inculcate habits of thrift and savings. The amount so saved is used for internal lending for 6 months. The SHG disburses consumption or productive loans. The mobilizers help in identification of Income Generating Activities (IGA). They help in opening a group savings account in the Bank. The members are encouraged to take up Microenterprises such as tailoring, goat rearing, operating a café or a grocery store, brick kiln, onion grading, beauty parlour. They have been able to repay their loans. Running such microenterprises, have given a sense of empowerment to women.

Self Employed Womens Association Ahemedabad

SEWA is a trade union registered in 1972. It is an organization of poor, self-employed women workers. These are women who earn a living through their own labor or small businesses. They do not have any regular salaried employment attached with welfare benefits; like workers in the organized sector. They are the unprotected labor force of our country.

Constituting 93% of the labor force, these are workers of the unorganized sector. Of the female labor force in India, more than 94% are in the unorganized sector. However their work is not counted and hence remains invisible.

There are as many as 26 SEWA sponsored cooperatives of all types:

- The SEWA Sahakari Bank.
- Abina, the Chindi Workers Cooperative.
- The Bann-san, the cane and bamboo workers cooperative.
- Aabodana the Handblock Printers Cooperative.
- Vijay and Utsah—the Weavers Cooperative.
- Matsyagandha—the Fish Vendors Cooperative.
- The service cooperatives comprising of paper pickers group.
- Saundarya, the cleaners cooperative.
- Livestock cooperatives.
- Land based cooperatives.
- Sangini—the child care cooperative.
- Jwala—the kerosene vendors cooperative.
- Trading and vending cooperatives.
- The carpenter's cooperative.
- The potters cooperative etc.

SEWA lays much emphasis on savings. It offers a number of saving schemes to it's members. The main needs come from ood, clothing and shelter. Some of its schemes and yojanas are the following:

Jivan Asha	Daily savings scheme
Chinta Nivaran Yojana	Worry Riddance Scheme
Mangal Prasang Yojana	Special Occasion scheme
Ghar Fund Yojana	House Fund Scheme
Kishori Gold Yojana	Buying Gold Scheme

SEWA has earned international recognition for its pioneering work in empowering women.

Financial Intermediary for Low Income

Bhagini Nivedita Sahakari Bank, Pune

Traditionally, banking and finance were perceived as the domain of men. Bhagin Nivedita Sahakari Bank is a bank run by women. Founded on 24th March, 1974, the chief promoter of the bank was Late Shri. Vivekrao Dadhe. He was by profession a chartered Accountant. The Bank was initially started in Ahmednagar as a cooperative bank. One section of this bank was run exclusively by women. Inspired by this, Shri Dadhe started a bank in Pune, which would be run exclusively by women.

Excusive Women Banks

These banks have only women member and are managed by women. Membership is open to men and women. 70% of members are women. By virtue of their structure, they have far better potential to bring about social transformation.

> *Low income people have shown that with responsive institutions, they can repay the loans and use their increased incomes and assets to transform their enterprises and their lives.*
>
> ***Nancy Berry, President, Women's World Banking***

Cooperatives have a tremendous potential to offer solutions to economic challenges and community development. Inclusive development has to be at the core of the development agenda. To this end we have to pursue time bound, non-discriminatory reforms that will give opportunities for women to be leaders in the next century.

CHAPTER 18

SHGs in Pune District

After the "green revolution" and the "white revolution" the country seems to be witnessing the "SHG revolution"; as Self Help Groups of the poor and the disadvantaged are formed across the country. 90% are comprised of only women members.

The SHG movement had its origin in Bangladesh, where Prof. Mohammad Yunus started lending small loans of 1 taka (Bangladesh Currency) to "poorest of the poor" women to start bamboo basket weaving livelihood activity. Soon the fame of "Grameen Bank" of Bangladesh reached over shores as the model became popular in other developing countries like the Banco Sol of Mexico. In February 1997 the World Micro Credit Summit was held in Washington DC. It announced a global target of supporting 100 million of the world's poorest families especially women with micro credit for self-employment.

The SHG-Bank linkage pilot project was initiated in 1992 in India, by NABARD. The estimated number of poor people assisted upto March 2003 was 58 million. Across India, the growth and promotion is larger in southern state of Andhra Pradesh, Karnataka and Tamil Nadu; in Mahrashtra there are a moderate number of SHGs. Considering the uneven growth of SHGs, the thrust is now developing SHGs in regions not covered so far. I had the opportunity of visiting some cooperative banks, which have successfully undertaken SHG financing in West Bengal and Bidar in Karnataka. The Andhra Pradesh Government has supported SHGs promoted by NGOs in their drought water shed management programmes.

The SHG movement holds the key to sustainable banking with poor. It is a participative process that helps in capacity building of the poor so as to enable them to take part in economic activities. The good performance in loan repayment has motivated banks to facilitate the formation of

SHGs. However, one must take care that the field staff is well equipped in nurturing the development of the SHGs, and do not succumb to pressure and hurry to meet the 'targets' to attract subsidy.

Through SHGs, capital is raised by its members, who are linked by a common bond like caste, sub-caste, community, place, origin or activity, age etc. SHGs start functioning with monthly meetings and collection of savings as decided by the group. They decide about small loan approvals and fixing terms of lending, saving, collection, and accounting of transactions. Surplus group savings are kept in the banks, and withdrawn in case of need. Each group is made upto 10 to 15 members and is based on self-help, self-responsibility, democracy, equality, equity and solidarity. It is an autonomous self-help organization, where members in their capacity as owners have the rights and obligations to participate in goal setting, decision-making, control and evaluation processes of their groups. The main objective of the self Help group are:

Mobilization of members thrift, and building up of group resources, Loan advancement to members for personal and business purposes, Orientation of members in the basics of financial management, and organizing and improving Mahila Multi-purpose cooperative societies, so as to increase the involvement of women in the primary agricultural cooperatives (PACs).

As the aim is all-round socio-economic development of the people, emphasis is on social issues as well, which includes: adult education/literacy programmes; health and family welfare; information about various agriculture activities; awareness of environmental protection; consumer protection and awareness, etc.

In the three talukas of Bhor, Velha and Haveli, in the Pune district, there are total of 160 SHGs. Enterprise training and marketing are two major obstacles in the development of SHGs. Various government agencies and NGOs are helping women to achieve sustainable and viable economic empowerment.

The SHGs managed by the Jijamata Research centre at shivpur, undertake various business activities by providing enterprise training to the members of the SHGs and product manufactured by them have even found a market in California, USA. The Shree Laxmi Group from Jategaon, Shikrapur is in existence since april 1997. It is supported by the KEM Research centre, Pabal.

The most potent tool against human deprivation is building the human capital among the deprived, through sustainable development initiatives. Today, this unique initiative in India of more than 2800 partners, has become a cost effective micro-finance initiative, enabling 11.6 million poor families to access sustainable financial services from the banking system through a network for a 7 lakh SHGs. The greatest challange however, lies in developing and sharing different level of conceptual and capacity building inputs with stakeholders.

Women today are increasingly being mobilized into Self Help Groups (SHGs) as a means to attain economic empowerment, which is the key to their success. Through SHGs, capital is raised by its members, who are linked by a common bond like caste, sub-caste, community, place, origin or activity, age, etc. SHGs start functioning with monthly meetings and collection of savings as decided by the group. They decide about small loan approval and fixing terms of lending, saving, collection and accounting of transactions. Surplus group savings are kept in the banks and withdrawn in case of need. Each group is made up of 10 to 15 members and is based on self-help, self-responsibility, democracy, equality, equity and solidarity. It is an autonomous self-help organization, where members in their capacity as owners have the rights and obligations to participate in goal setting, decision-making, control and evaluation processes of their groups. The main objectives of the Self Help Group are:

- Mobilization of member's thrift and building up of group's resources.
- Loan advancement to members personal and business purposes.
- Orientation of members in financial management.
- Organising and improving Mahila Multi-purposes Cooperative Societies so as to increase the involvement of women in the Primary Agricultural Cooperatives (PACs).
- As the aim is socio-economic development of the people, emphasis is on social development as well, which includes:
- Adult education/Literacy programmes
- Health and family welfare
- Information about various agricultural activities
- Awareness of environmental protection
- Consumer protection awareness, etc.

Conclusion

The most potent tool against human deprivation is building the human capital among the deprived, through sustainable development initiatives. Today this unique initiative in India of more than 2800 partners has become a cost effective microfinance initiative in the world enabling 11.6 million poor families to access sustainable financial services from the banking system through a network of over 112 lakhs SHGs. The greatest challenge lies in developing and sharing different levels of conceptual and capacity building inputs with the stakeholders.

CHAPTER 19

Integrate Tenets of Self-Help Groups in State-Financed Schemes

(Successful project need replicating on a larger scale)

Microfinance has emerged as in instrument of poverty alleviation by way of providing credit and other financial services to the poor. It has been promoted by linking self-help groups (SHGs) of the poor with banks either directly or through non-government organizations (NGOs).

Although India has the largest banking network in the world, with a branch for every 15,000 rural households and a cooperative in almost every village, the share of the formal financial sector in total rural credit usage is 57%, compared with about 43% for informal finance. It is estimated that India has nearly 400 million people living below the poverty line. Approximately 75 million household need microfinance, of which nearly 60 million households are in rural areas and 15 million are urban slumdwellers.

On the supply side, the number of small loan accounts from banks covers only about 40 million households (of the 75 million), leaving 35 million out of the purview of the formal system to manage their resources from the informal sector.

It is evident that there is wide gap between demand and formal sector's limited supply. India is perhaps the largest emerging market for micro financial services in the world. The National Bank for Agriculture and Rural Development (Nabard) has a set a target for banks to extend loans to one million SHGs by 2008.

A high-powered committee was set up by Nabard to work out a conceptual framework for a national policy on micro-finance, for mainstreaming micro-finance institutions and to suggest an inter-institutional framework. The requirements of micro credit were estimated Rs. 15,000–50,000 crore per year. Against this, bank advances to weaker sections aggregated to Rs. 9,700 crore, suggesting a huge gap in the provision of financial services to the poor.

It is in this backdrop that 'banking with the poor' has to be made possible through priority sector lending. SHG-bank linkages and lending by banks and financial institutions to micro-finance institutions. The task force recommended issues like promotion and growth of micro-finance through SHGs and other innovative credit delivery models. It also emphasized that the basic tenets of SHGs should be assimilated in government-sponsored schemes.

In the formal not-for-profit sector, the agencies involved in promoting SHGs are government agencies, viz., District Rural Development Agency (DRDA), cooperative, panchayat raj, Nabard, NGOs etc. The for-profit MFIs include rural non-banking finance companies like BASIX, SHARE and commercial banks like ICICI, GTB and companies like Hindustan Lever, which are looking at micro-finance as a profitable activity.

Financial services will have to be integrated with broader issues like enhancing incomes, promoting alternative livelihood, soil and water conservation, livestock development and diversification of agriculture, horticulture which can trigger non-farm employment, with secondary and tertiary benefits. Spontaneous and innovative efforts of SHGs can lead to dispersed and decentralized development.

Till now the government has played a peripatetic role and the impact on development has been marginal. In 1980–81, the government established the Integrated Rural Development Programme (IRDP) to direct subsidized loans to poor self employed people through banks. It extended assistance to about 55 million families. But the programme could not be sustained. A major drawback of government departments was the lack of orientation towards targeting of loans which led to inappropriate choice of beneficiaries.

Strategies need to be worked out to establish a range of linkages. One needs to take a holistic view of development, and a more balanced pattern of spatial and sustainable development. Adequate income and employment schemes exist in rural areas, but they need to be tapped the right way. Successful projects need to be replicated on a large scale; possibly a core group with regional committees could work on this.

SHG training and advocacy seems to be a bandwagon that everyone wants to jump on to without understanding the issues involved. There seems to be no dearth of institutions at the regional or state level that want to do SHG training. Inevitably, a 'numbers game' is being played. Who can reach more participants? Who can scale up the fastest? There is no impact analysis or a follow-up on training. Moreover, quantity most often takes precedence over quality as targets are imposed.

In a round of training programmes designed to sensitise government functionaries in Maharashtra, many suggestions came up. For instance, while for panchyat raj and gram sabha training institutes the need is strengthen infrastructure, financial and human resources, DRDA project directors need technical and marketing inputs. The cooperation department needs inputs on strengthening internal governance and district industries centres need inputs on micro-enterprise development.

For the widest and most sustainable impact, all these stakeholders need to be brought on a common platform. Partnering with expert agencies would enable them to share experiences. Further, academic material like case studies, innovations at MFOs, new learning methods and research could be fostered.

Bibliography

Books

Acharya, S. (1987). Women and Rural Development in the Third World, Bombay, Tata Institute of Social Sciences.

ADB (2000). "Finance for the poor: microfinance development strategy", Manila, ADB 3.

Ahmad, Ansari Saghir (2007). "Microfinance in India", Asian Economic Review, 49(2): 327–336.

Ahmed, Rais, Microfinance and Women Empowerment (Part 3), a Mittal publication.

Alka, Srivastava, "Women's Self Help Groups: Findings from a Study in Four Indian States", *Social Change*, Vol. 35, No. 2, June 2005.

Anand, "High Cost of finance in Microcredit Business in Andhra Pradesh (India): Problems and Possible Solutions", *The ICFAIAN Journal of Management Research*, Vol. 7, No. 4, 2008.

Basu and Srivastava, "Scaling-up Microfinance for India's Rural Poor", World Bank Policy Research Working Paper – 3646, January, 2006, Available from: http://www.worldbank.ord.

Beyond Micro-Credit Putting Development Back into Microfinance, Vista Publications, New Delhi, 2007.

Centre for microfinance research (2006). "Microfinance in India current trends and challenges".

Chandra, Tulika, "Institutional Support for Women Empowerment in India—Special Reference to Mahila Cooperative Bank", *Indian Cooperative Review*, Vol. 45, No. 3, January 2008.

Chandrakavate, M.S., "The SHGs Model of Microfinance: A Silent Movement Towards Empowering Rural Women", *Southern Economist*, January 1, 2006.

Chhatoi, Shanti and Nayak (2009). "Financing the poor through SHG-bank linkage programme", *The Indian journal of commerce*, Vol. 62, No. 1, Jan.–March, 2009.

Das, S.K., Nanda, B.P. and Rathi, J. (2009). Microfinance and Rural Development in India, New Century Publication, New Delhi.

Dasgupta and Rajaram, "Microfinance in India: Empirical Evidence, Alternative Models and Policy Imperatives", *Economic and Political Weekly*, 19 March, 2005.

Dasgupta, R. (2001). "Working and Impact of Rural Self-Help Groups and other Forms of Microfinancing: An Informal Journey through Self-Help Groups", *Indian Journal of Agricultural Economics*, 56(3), 370–386.

Dasgupta, R. (2005). "Microfinance in India: Empirical evidence, alternative models and policy imperatives", *Economic and Political Weekly*, 60(12):1229–1237.

Dearaja, T.D., University of Mysore, Hassan (2011), Microfinance in India—A tool for Poverty Reduction.

Dubhashi, P.R., "Principles and Philosophy of Cooperation", *Vaikunth Mehta National Institute of Cooperative Management*, 1970.

Fernandez, Aloysius Prakash, The Myrada Experience Alternate Management Systems for Savings and Credit of the Rural Poor.

Feroze, S.M. and Chauhan, A.K., "Microfinance in India: A Performance Evaluation (Including a Case Study of Haryana)".

Gandhi, Sharma and Maheshwari (2009). "Escaping Poverty in Rural Mewat – Case Studies from an Integrated Approach", *Research Bulletin*, No 1, IRRAD Publications.

Gaonkar, Rekha R. (2004). "Role of Self-help Groups in empowerment of Women", *Paper Presented in ISTR Sixth International Conference*, Toronto, Canada, 11–14th July.

Gender Equality—Empowerment of Rural Women through NABARD Schemes, NABARD, Mumbai.

History of Microfinance (2009). Retrieved at http://www.microfiannceinfo.com/history-of-microfinance.

Indian Microfinance—The Challenges of Rapid Growth, SAGE Publications Pvt. Ltd., New Delhi, 2007.

Karmakar, K.G. (1999). Rural credit and self-Help Groups-Microfinance.

Karmakar, K.G., "Rural Credit and Self-help groups: Microfinance Needs and Concepts in India", Sage Publications, New Delhi 1999.

Kishanjit, Badu and Krishan, Jindal, "Microfinance Emerging Challenges", TATA McGRAW HILL, New Delhi, 2000.

Mayoux, Linda, Sustainable Learning for Women's Empowerment Ways Forward in Micro-Finance.

Micro-Credit Poverty and Empowerment linking the Triad, SAGE Publications Pvt. Ltd., New Delhi, 2005.

Microfinance in India, SAGE Publications Pvt. Ltd., New Delhi, 2008.

Mishra, S.N. and Hossain, M.M. (2001). "A Study on the Working and Impact of Dharmadevi Mahila Mandal: A Rural Self Help Group in Kalahandi District of Orissa", *Indian Journal of Agricultural Economics*, Vol. 56, No. 3, pp. 480–81.

NABARD, Annual Report 2010–11.

NABARD, Status of Microfinance in India Report, 2014–15.

National Conference on Financial Inclusion and beyond, www.microfinancegateway.org

Pitt and Khandkar, "Grameen Bank, Bangladesh Rural Advancement Committee RD12", Progoti Publishers, Bangladesh, 1995.

Priya, Basu and Pradeep, Srivastava, "Exploring Possibilities Microfinance and Rural Credit Access for the Poor in India", *Economic & Political Weekly*, April 23, 2005.

Rao, S.N. Hanumantha, Chairman, Deccan Grameen Bank, Hyderabad. Total Financial Inclusion—A success story.

Sharma, M. (2010). Index of Financial Inclusion, Discussion Papers in Economics, CITD, School of International Studies, JNU.

SHGs: A study of selected districts in Orissa and Haryana", *Journal of rural development*, ISSN 0970-3357, Vol. 29, No. 2, April–June, 2010, pp. 157–171.

Singh, S.K. and Pandey, S.P. (2008). Empowerment of Women through Self-help Groups, serial Publication, New Delhi.

Sivakumar, V. and Balbir, B. Bhasin (2009). Path to Financial Inclusion: The success of Self-Help Groups-Bank Linkage Programme in India, *International Business and Economics Research Journal*, 8(11).

Small Enterprise Development—An International Journal of Microfinance and Business Development, Volume 12, Number 1, March 2001, Theme issue: Microinsurance ITDG Publishing.

Status of Microfinance in India, 2010–11.

The Economics of Microfinance, Prentice-Hall of India, New Delhi, 2007.

Thorat Usha (2007a). Taking Banking Services to the Common Man-financial Inclusion, Deputy Governor, Reserve Bank of India at the HMT-DFID Financial Inclusion Conference 2007, Whitehall Place, London, UK, June 19.

Tripathy, K.K. and Jain, S.K. (2010). "Microfinance and rural self employment through

Reports of NABARD

1. Status of Microfinance in India, NABARD, Mumbai, 2016–2017.
2. Status of Microfinance in India, NABARD, Mumbai, 2017–2018.
3. Status of Microfinance in India, NABARD, Mumbai, 2018–2019.
4. Status of Microfinance in India, NABARD, Mumbai, 2019–2020.
5. Status of Microfinance in India, NABARD, Mumbai 2020–2021.

Websites Referred

www.developmentgateway.com
www.drda.ap.org
www.indiastat.com
www.mda.nic.in
www.mewat.gov.in
www.microfinance.com
www.microfinance.india
www.microfinancegateway.org/content/article
www.microfinanceindia.org
www.nabard.org
www.nabard.org.
www.ruralpovertyportal.org.
www.serp.ap.org
www.shodhganga.inflibnet.ac.in
www.wikipedia.org

www.ingramcontent.com/pod-product-compliance
Lightning Source LLC
Chambersburg PA
CBHW071445230926
51846CB00001B/347
* 9 7 8 9 3 9 0 9 5 1 3 2 1 *